THE BEST
WORLD WAR I
STORY I KNOW

ON THE POINT IN THE ARGONNE

THE BEST
WORLD WAR I
STORY I KNOW

ON THE POINT IN THE ARGONNE

SEPTEMBER 26–OCTOBER 16, 1918

NIMROD T. FRAZER

ISBN: 978-1-7325485-0-3 - Paperback
eISBN: 978-1-7325485-1-0 - ePub
eISBN: 978-1-7325485-1-0 - mobi

Library of Congress Control Number: 2018951301

Printed in the United States of America   0 7 1 2 1 8

♾ This paper meets the requirements of ANSI/NISO Z39.48-1992 (Permanence of Paper)

Photographs for the photo-montage on the book cover courtesy of National Archives, 111-SC- 23918 and 28382. It depicts Brigadier General MacArthur, Colonel Bare, Capitaine Drouhin in a staff meeting with the Côte de Châtillon in the background.

A detailed account of how American military forces finally succeeded in breaking through the famous Hindenburg Line to end WWI. I am proud of the role the 42nd ID played in key Meuse-Argonne battles, especially their victory at the Côte de Châtillon, which proved to be the Division's most difficult battle of the war.

–Major General Steven Ferrari
CG, 42nd Infantry Division

CONTENTS

LIST OF MAPS

All maps created by Alexander Fries, The University of Alabama Cartographic Research Lab

LIST OF PHOTOGRAPHS

PREFACE

The importance of teaching history cannot be denied, both because, as the famous philosopher George Santayana said, "Those who cannot remember the past are condemned to repeat it," but also because history is the message that needs be passed on to young generations to root them in their humanity and help them understand that they are part of our chain of transmission, of our future but also our past.

As an archaeologist and an educator, I have always been fascinated by history, eager to transmit its lessons and to remember those who made history, the well-known as well as the unknown, the heroes as well as the simple protagonists. Their lives give a meaning to mine, a sense of belonging to mankind as a whole, beyond borders and timelines.

Twenty-five years ago, on an archaeological journey to the Middle East, supporting the American Schools of Oriental Research, I met businessman Nimrod T. Frazer. In Palmyra, he told me his father had fought in France during World War I (WWI). He also told me his father had been an alcoholic. This didn't surprise me, as WWI was one of the most inhumane times of human history, and most soldiers returned home with deep psychological trauma. We spoke at length about the war, and it made me realize how little Americans knew or remembered about it, a war in which they lost more men in six months of combat than in Korea and Vietnam put together. This war placed the United States on the world stage and profoundly transformed our country economically, socially, and scientifically.

This was one hundred years ago, and we are still living in the shadows of its consequences. How could we have stopped teaching about WWI? How can we understand World War II (WWII) and our American century if we don't start with WWI? How can we understand what our forefathers went through if we don't know how brutal it was?

This was what Frazer endeavored to do, to understand his father and overcome the memory of growing up with an alcoholic father. I supported him in all aspects of this endeavor, in the research for his first book, in acquiring the land in where today stands a memorial to the Rainbow Division on the grounds where his father received a purple heart, in introducing him to the great James Butler, Member of the Royal Academy, who sculpted the Rainbow Soldier statue. A twin statue of the Rainbow Memorial stands today in front of Montgomery's Union Station, and Butler also sculpted the bronze Daedalus placed at Maxwell Air Force Base to commemorate the entry of the American air service in WWI, a reminder also of the role of aviation in Montgomery's history.

Frazer wanted to continue bringing back to life the soldiers of WWI, his father's comrades and the men who inspired his personal commitment to service, his own combat in Korea. In following the path of the 42nd Division in *Send the Alabamians*, he had discovered that the Côte de Châtillon, a linchpin on the Kriemhilde Stellung, the famous German defensive line, had been the objective first of the 35th Division, then of the 1st Division, whose combat record had been admirable. The 1st Division's courage and sacrifice in the Argonne appeared lesser-known than its previous actions in Cantigny and Soissons, probably because by then so many more American divisions were engaged in combat and garnered as much attention.

Such a story was definitely worth telling, which is how this new book came to life. By then, I was serving on the US World War I Centennial Commission (WWICC) based on my record as President of the Croix Rouge Farm Memorial Foundation, focused on commemorating WWI, and on my tenure for six years as President of the International Baccalaureate Organization, whose roots are in the International School of Geneva, created in the aftermath of WWI to educate the children of the League of Nations delegates and staff.

As a WWI Centennial Commissioner, with a responsibility for international and educational projects, I came to meet Damien Georges, an extraordinary gentleman, a forestry man in charge of some of the French national forests in the Ardennes, a region which saw so much bloodshed during both World Wars. He had lived in those woods for decades, knew them like the back of his hand, and loved them as much as all the animals and the plants that lived in them. He also constantly remembered the men from far away who had come and given their life in a fight for peace. He instigated an extraordinary project, with the full support of his colleagues in the National Office of Forestry (ONF), and, with the help of local high school students, planted 1700 trees in the shape of the First Division coat of arms, to remember the division's 1700 soldiers who gave their lives there in the service of France one hundred years ago.

I was well-acquainted with Nimrod Frazer's interest in the 1st Division history in this last offensive of WWI, and my meeting with the ONF, to which I presented the WWICC's endorsement for this project, made me ask Frazer to finish his book in time for the inauguration of the historical trails the ONF planned for the centennial of the Meuse-Argonne campaign. Concurrently, I suggested that the ONF enlarge its project from only the 1st Division to the 35th and the 42nd Divisions, who succeeded each other in that particular offensive to capture the Côte de Châtillon. Some of their leaders in this action are not forgotten today: Harry Truman, 33rd United States president; the famous George Patton, who was injured serving with the 35th Division on the first day of the offensive; "Wild" Bill Donovan, who earned a Medal of Honor there and would then create the OSS, the precursor of the CIA; as well as Douglas MacArthur, whose 84th Brigade captured the Côte de Châtillon and who would continue to distinguish himself in WWII and during the Korean War.

This is how the ONF's wonderful project came to exist as it stands today, encompassing the history of these three divisions in the region, with an orientation table on the high point of Cornay from which one can view most of the Meuse-Argonne battlefield; a historical and botanical trail around the 1st Division coat of arms, a "Shroud Forest," as the French have baptized it; and a plaque to honor MacArthur on a small monument, facing the Côte de Châtillon, made of stones from the old Tuilerie Farm, an important part of his offensive.

This book therefore is not only a tribute to the soldiers from these three divisions but also a guide to the ONF WWI memorial trail in the Ardennes. It stands there to bring to life the American soldiers' deeds and help new generations understand their service and sacrifice.

I wish to end this preface with the words from another forester, Jacques Baudelot, Director of the ONF in the Ardennes, who wrote me after a group of 1st Division soldiers visited the trail in May 2018:

> My first gratitude goes to the veterans who are not with us anymore and who sadly remain in the Argonne forever, allowing that through their sacrifice we can today be free men, standing tall. The presence of these soldiers that you accompanied during the visit of the ONF memorial trail overwhelmed the man that I am today, who, especially during the visit of the centennial plantation, became fully aware of the nobility of our common action and its scope. The protocol would not have allowed it, therefore I kept inside of me the tears that invaded me in front of these young soldiers. Their presence was a better reminder than any speech could have done that a hundred years ago, the same men had been present but at the time to give up their life for an ideal that we must continue to defend, that of peace and respect for certain values, including freedom.

Monique B. Seefried, Ph.D.
Commissioner
U.S. World War I Centennial Commission

ACKNOWLEDGEMENTS

Dr. Monique B. Seefried is much too modest in her preface. She was the one who first suggested my writing two books about World War I and guided me through the process. She brought scholarly discipline and introduced me to most of the people outside of Alabama that I would like to now thank for their contribution to my research and the publication of this book.

Foremost on this list is Dr. Mitchell Yockelson from the National Archives, who helped me over the years in my research and contributed significantly to the completion of this book on the 35th, 1st, and 42nd Divisions at the end of WWI.

I would also like to thank Jonathan Casey and Doran Cart at the World War I Museum in Kansas City; Paul Herbert, Mary Manning, and Andrew Woods at the First Division Museum at Cantigny; James Zobel at the MacArthur Memorial and Archives in Norfolk; Genoa R. Stanford at the MCoE HQ Donovan Research Library; and Frank Hanner, the former director of the National Infantry Museum at Fort Benning, for supporting me during my visits to their respective institutions and guiding my research there.

At West Point, I was fortunate to receive the support of Col. Gail Yoshitani in the Department of History, who introduced me to the USMA Library Special Collection team to continue my research. West Point Historian Sherman Fleek also provided important information.

In France itself, Damien Georges from the National Office of Forestry; Jean-Pierre Brouillon, the owner of the land around the Côte de Châtillon; and David Bedford from the American Battle Monuments Commission (ABMC) shared with me maps, photographs, and their invaluable knowledge of the terrain.

Jean Paul Amat, professor of biogeography at the University of Paris Sorbonne, had the kindness of reading my manuscript and offering important geographical suggestions.

In Alabama, I was fortunate to benefit from the continuous support of Steve Murray, Director of the state of Alabama Department of Archives and History. I also want to especially thank

Donna Baker from the University of Alabama Press, whose commitment, experience, guidance, and contribution were essential to the publication of this book. She introduced me to Elizabeth Wade, editor of this book, who had previously worked so successfully with me on *Send the Alabamians* and who kept the process moving at a critical time. To both of them, I am exceedingly grateful. I also wish to thank Alex Fries, from The University of Alabama Cartographic Research Lab, for his important contribution.

These acknowledgements would not be complete without thanking Major General (ret.) Joseph Taluto and Brigadier General (ret.) Paul Genereux, who granted me the honor of having my book published by the Rainbow Division Veterans Foundation. Nothing could have been more pleasing to my father and his comrades, who fought so well and so successfully in that division during WWI.

INTRODUCTION

My father, Will Frazer, was a sergeant with Gen. Douglas MacArthur's brigade of "Alabama cotton-pickers and Iowa corn-growers"—the men who finally took the Côte de Châtillon on October 16, 1918.[1] Army lore holds that soldiers in combat find the danger of death less threatening than physical hardships. Most believed that death was for somebody else, but the exhaustion, rain, cold, mud, and lice did not retreat from them or their memory. My father remembered these things vividly, along with the hills, the sacrifices, and the hard year of fighting that culminated with the Côte de Châtillon's capture.

I grew up with my old man's stories and wrote a history of Alabama's 167th Infantry Regiment in the 42nd Division, called the "Rainbow" Division.[2] As part of my research, I spent years digging into accounts of the 1918 events leading to the capture of the Côte de Châtillon. These events, known as the Meuse-Argonne offensive, commenced on September 26, 1918. The campaign was a huge affair—much bigger than previous American Western Front battles. Under Gen. John J. Pershing's 1st US Army, the opening attack consisted of fifteen US Army divisions organized as three corps (the I, II, and III Corps) on the line.[3] Each American corps had three divisions in the assault position on the front line, a division in support of the front-line division, and a division in reserve. An American division had almost 28,000 officers and men, twice the size of Allied and German divisions. American soldiers were affectionately known as doughboys, a moniker dating back to the 1846-48 Mexican War. In addition to tanks and artillery pieces, France offered its Second Colonial Corps, the six divisions of the Seventeenth Army Corps, and the 5th Cavalry Division to be placed in reserve.[4]

The Meuse-Argonne was the main objective of the right wing of Field Marshal Ferdinand Foch's grand allied offensive. Foch, who had the overarching coordination of the Allied armies, sought to push the Germans back into Germany. As part of his plan, the 1st US

Army was to attack with the French 4th Army on its left and advance to the towns of Sedan and Mezières, which held important rail lines.[5] The men faced German defensive lines running east–west. Though such lines were typical, in the Meuse-Argonne they were closer together than on other fronts, placed that way with wire, machine gun nests, and deep trenches to provide maximum protection for the vital railroad line from Sedan to Metz.

The Germans used the area's natural landscape to their advantage, transforming many hills into German fortified strongpoints from which they combatted American progress through lower terrain. German defensive positions were well organized, with both natural and manmade features. All were served by communication trenches and bunkers. Some were concrete pill boxes and machine gun nests constructed over four years of German occupation. Among these hills, Hill 260, or the Côte de Châtillon, stood on the highest ground and controlled lines of fire all around, making it a key stronghold on the Meuse-Argonne front that the Germans intended to hold at all costs.

The Côte de Châtillon was also significant because it stood as a strongpoint along the Kriemhilde Stellung, a linchpin of the German Hindenburg Line. Constructed during the winter of 1916–1917, the Hindenburg Line protected troops and supply systems. Because it ran over 100 kilometers to the German border, the line connected German forces to Germany itself. The Hindenburg Line was made up of three or four different lines of defense that in some places had up to fifteen trench lines.[6] In this area, the Hindenburg Line consisted of four main lines of defense. One covered the area from Vienne-le-Chateau to Regnéville-sur-Meuse. The Giselher Stellung, the second one, included Montfaucon. The third and most formidable one, the Kriemhilde Stellung, encompassed the heights of Romagne, Cunel, and the village of Grandpré. The fourth and weakest one, the Freya Stellung, stood to the north.[7]

Because of the Côte de Châtillon's significant and strategic location, taking it became an important part of Foch's plan. Its capture during what Americans referred to as the first two phases of the Meuse-Argonne campaign enabled the American advance towards

Sedan, the final objective of the third phase of the battles. However, securing the Côte de Châtillon proved a formidable task, requiring three successive divisions—the 35th, the 1st, and the 42nd. After the 35th suffered early setbacks that called into question the entire fate of the American war effort, the 1st and 42nd Divisions labored to take the hill and earn hard-won success. The history of how these three divisions managed such a feat is the best story I know from WWI.

This account begins with the jump-off of the green and untried 35th Division, a National Guard unit from Kansas and Missouri. Ambitious orders called for it to take the Côte de Châtillon quickly,[8] but the division's poor organization and lack of experience proved too detrimental. Bloodied and badly broken, the 35th failed to take the hill, and Pershing pulled the division from the front.

The story then turns to the Regular Army 1st Division—the best fighting unit in the American Army, sometimes called the "Red One" or "The Big Red One," nicknames that have endured. Soldiers in the 1st served in extraordinary ways, but their record in the Argonne was sometimes eclipsed by their earlier accomplishments at Cantigny and Soissons, where they stopped the Germans in some of the Americans' first Western Front battles. In the Meuse-Argonne offensive, the 1st Division replaced the defeated 35th, taking over its mission on the point and continuing until every one of its infantry units was used up. The 1st Division fought very well, but its men were exhausted from prior campaigns, and it lacked enough men to keep going. For ten days the 1st Division tried to capture the Côte de Châtillon, but it was eventually clear that fresh troops were needed.

Meanwhile, other divisions on the Argonne front were struggling to advance, prompting Pershing to write, "The period of battle, between October 1st to the 11th, involved the heaviest strain on the army and on me."[9] But Pershing refused to give up, deciding instead to send the 42nd Rainbow Division against the Côte de Châtillon. The division attacked, was driven back, then continued attacking.

Here Douglas MacArthur first established his reputation as a military commander and accelerated his career, which would encompass two more wars before ending in 1952. When the Rainbow Division's 83rd Brigade failed to capture the Côte de Châtillon,

MacArthur's 84th Brigade—a regiment of Alabamians, a regiment of Iowans, and a machine gun battalion from Georgia—was ordered to take the hill. They succeeded on October 16, taking and holding the important German position when almost none believed it could be done with only one brigade.[10]

This book relates simple facts about men and units in constant combat over a three-week period. This description of vicious fighting includes the failure of every infantry element of a division (the 35th), the failure of the army's best division to reach its final objective (the 1st), and the failure of a brigade of the army's best National Guard Division (the 42nd Division's 83rd Brigade). All these failures happened despite great acts of courage that often involved many casualties.

Some, but not all, accounts of the campaign are well-known by historians, but they are mostly unknown by the public at large. My intention has been to present readers with a large variety of authentic situations taken from regimental histories, military citations, diaries and personal letters, and available literature, including works written by experts on the Meuse-Argonne offensive.

The story relies heavily on the essays written in the 1920s and 1930s for Advanced Courses of the Infantry School at Ft. Benning, Georgia, by men who were lieutenants, captains, and majors in the Meuse-Argonne offensive.[11] This Infantry School collection, held at the Fort Benning Donovan Library, vividly describes the 35th Division's collapse. It contains rich materials concerning the 1st Division's hard fighting around Exermont and Fléville, its crossing of Cote 240, and its attack on and defense of Cote 272 at the base of the Côte de Châtillon. The collection also describes the successful but costly attack that MacArthur and the Rainbow Division made against the same hill. Though there were many heroics to be praised in these events, the accounts offer an unflinching portrait of the reality of war, as they also detail instances of cowardice and tell of men who died from untreated wounds.

In addition to these first-person accounts from the Infantry School collection, my work draws on material from officers and general officers' correspondence in the West Point archives. In this correspondence, Pershing gives guidance in the matter of an officer shooting an American soldier running in the face of the enemy. The archival materials also examine how Pershing held corps commanders responsible for failure of individual soldiers in their units. It contains German intelligence assessments of Americans in combat, and it details the sacking of brigadier generals and field grade officers (majors through general officers).

My research relies also on participants' replies to the Army War College Veterans surveys; records kept by archives, libraries, and historical societies; and letters, diaries, and other firsthand accounts, including books written by soldiers who survived the war.

Of course, readers may gain additional insight from visiting the numerous WWI historical and memorial sites in France. Therefore, this text serves as both a history of the three-week period leading to the Americans' capture of the Côte de Châtillon and as a travel handbook with maps for those who visit the battlefields of the Argonne, a succession of forests, valleys, and wetlands.[12]

Among the men who fought at the Côte de Châtillon were some who later played important roles in US history, including battery commander Harry S. Truman, tank officer George S. Patton, battalion commander William Donovan, and operations officer George C. Marshall. Many lesser-known individuals who participated in the campaign would also assume important roles in the US economy, in domestic affairs following WWI, and in the US Army during World War II (WWII). Other combatants returned to their regular lives, though many came back broken and troubled by their combat experience. This book pays homage to all of them and most especially to the three thousand Americans killed in this part of the Meuse-Argonne offensive. Their sacrifice should never be forgotten.

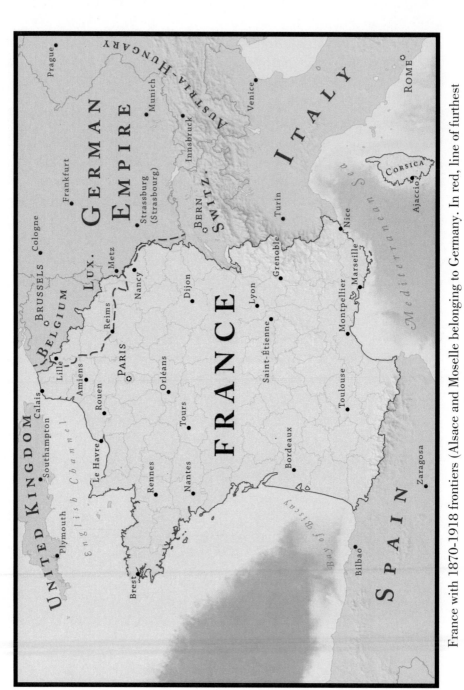

France with 1870-1918 frontiers (Alsace and Moselle belonging to Germany. In red, line of furthest advance, July 18, 1918.)

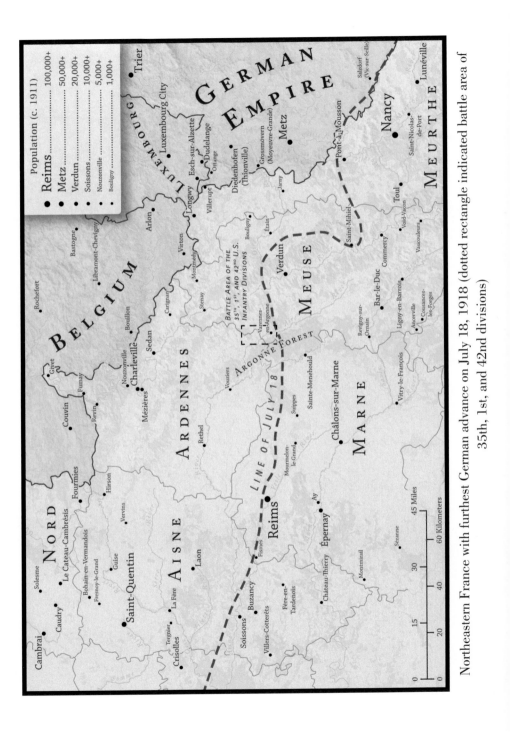

Northeastern France with furthest German advance on July 18, 1918 (dotted rectangle indicated battle area of 35th, 1st, and 42nd divisions)

CHAPTER 1

The Meuse-Argonne campaign and the 35th Division

Americans in combat

By the summer of 1918 British and French forces were exhausted from losing nearly two million men during four years of war against "German soldiers who fought on with grim determination."[13] The 1917 battles in Verdun, the Somme, and Ypres—where they participated in repeated operations—decimated their ranks, and replacements were slim. American troops were the answer. The United Stated entered the war in April 1917, and the first US troops arrived in June 1917. Though only four divisions were in France by the end of that year, by the next spring Americans poured into the Western Front in great number—more than 100,000 a month. On May 28, 1918, elements of the 1st Division took part in the first large-scale American attack when Cantigny was captured and held.

In July Germany launched its Peace Offensive, an all-out effort to defeat the Allies and force peace. German high command believed it would win the war with reinforcements released from the Eastern Front after the Russians stopped fighting alongside the Allies. Timing was of the essence, though, because from July 1918 onwards, 250,000 Americans arrived in France every month.[14]

The French asked the Americans to help stop the German attack, which threatened to reach a position approximately fifty-five miles from Paris. General Pershing placed several American divisions under French command there. In mid-July, Gen. Henri Gouraud's 4th French Army, in which the US 42nd Rainbow Division distinguished itself, helped halt the Germans in the Champagne region. The German high command now recognized that Americans were both willing to fight and able to hold ground taken from their first-class troops.[15]

Meanwhile, French and British confidence in the Americans grew.[16] Supreme Allied Commander Marshal Ferdinand Foch, who commanded all the Allied troops, recognized his new opportunity to counterattack and immediately launched a series of battles involving the 1st, 2nd (including the 5th and 6th US Marine regiments), 3rd, and 4th US Army Divisions. Nearly all succeeded. By September the Americans were ready to fight as an American Army under American command. They had prepared to attack the Germans in the sector of St. Mihiel, which was blocking the road to Metz, the important French military town captured by the Germans in 1870 during the Franco-Prussian War. Three American corps of about 400,000 US troops and 48,000 French took up positions on the night of September 11, and St. Mihiel was taken from 75,000 retreating Germans on September 13.[17] This one-sided battle was over on September 16, 1918.[18]

Twelve American divisions, only four of which had experienced previous combat, achieved quick and easy victory at St. Mihiel.[19] Along with some possible hubris, the glow of success inspired Pershing's forces. With light losses, the war's first large "All American" operation (meaning that it was directed by an American command with support of some French troops) would be remembered as a "cake walk" by some Americans.[20] However, many others experienced their first smell of gunfire at St. Mihiel. This was psychologically important despite the fact that the battle was a minor strategic event.[21] An experienced 1st Division officer, Barnwell Legge, participated in the offensive. Later, when speaking of the recently victorious but green US Army, he suggested that "The psychological effect of a rapid and successful advance of a large army over thirteen kilometers, with practically no losses, had an astounding effect upon those men."[22]

Pershing now believed his army had mastered its logistical, planning, and training problems,[23] but that would be put to a greater test fewer than ten days after the St. Mihiel attack concluded, when Pershing's 1st Army had to be in line for the September 26 jump-off for the Meuse-Argonne operation.

By then the Allies were close enough to the German border to believe they might drive the retreating Germans out of France, thereby accomplishing one of Foch's central goals. But the German Army was determined and committed to defending the conquered coal fields of Northern France and Belgium. Along with the iron mines of Lorraine, those captured riches were essential to the German war effort, as they fueled the production of equipment and ammunition.[24] The Americans had two primary roles: to thwart German communication and shake German confidence. If the Germans retreated the Americans were to cut their rail supply lines and expose their armies to capture. Meanwhile, the large numbers of arriving Americans ensured that the Germans could not claim the rapid victory they desired.

The Meuse-Argonne region

Foch had originally planned for the Meuse-Argonne battle to be fought in 1919, but the timing was changed to fall 1918 after the French and British victories during the Second Battle of the Marne and Amiens. American divisions supported those battles, and after the Americans' easy win at St. Mihiel, the plan was altered to move them toward the Argonne immediately.[25] As Pvt. Donald Kyler, a soldier in the 16th Infantry Regiment wrote in his memoirs, "The Meuse Argonne was a larger operation than St. Mihiel, but it was treated as a continuation of the earlier battle. The same troops fought in both. St. Mihiel was over but a short time when fighting in the Argonne started."[26]

The offensive would be fought in a sector between the Meuse River and the dense Argonne Forest in northern France. The terrain featured a series of steep hills and porous rock. Heavy rain, which fell frequently in autumn, formed chains of ponds and lakes. Clay soil that easily turned to mud blanketed the forest. Combined with the area's dense trees, all this made the ground difficult to traverse.[27]

The plan was to create a huge strategic Allied campaign, one that fully involved the French and the British in the north. It would become the Americans' largest and most complex operation in the war, over an area about eighteen miles east-west. More American troops—1.2 million—were required in that single operation than at any other point in American history before or since.[28]

The Germans expected the coming American attack to be at Metz, a major rail center northeast of St. Mihiel. Fighting in the Argonne would require the Americans to relocate much of the 1st US Army, and the move from the St. Mihiel to the Meuse-Argonne was twice as long as the move between St. Mihiel and the Metz front.[29] Gen. Max von Gallwitz, the German commander, did not believe Pershing would take a longer route than was absolutely necessary to fight a major battle. The Germans reinforced Metz, placing five divisions in line between the Meuse River and the Argonne plateau.

Despite his confidence, Gallwitz was mistaken. US Infantry units began the move towards the Argonne from St. Mihiel on September 19, 1918.[30] Half a million soldiers and support elements had to travel more than sixty miles over three roads, two of them reserved for wagons, trucks, and artillery. This was the first major move of artillery pieces pulled by motor vehicle and of some ammunition moved by special motor trucks. Traffic jams and delays took place, but they accomplished the move in two weeks.[31] To keep the Germans believing that Metz was the target, the men marched at night, often in the rain. The ruse worked, as German observation planes completely failed to see the troops marching at night or hiding during the day.

Before the battle, approximately 600,000 Americans moved into the front.[32] The order of battle placed I Corps on the left with the 77th, 28th, and 35th Divisions; V Corps in the center with the 91st, 37th, and 79th Divisions; and III Corps on the right with the 4th, 80th, and 33rd Divisions.[33] Three divisions were in reserve.

Table 1, Order of Battle

I Corps	V Corps	III Corps
77th Division	91st Division (inexperienced)	4th Division
28th Division	37th Division (inexperienced)	80th Division
35th Division (inexperienced)	79th Division (inexperienced)	33rd Division

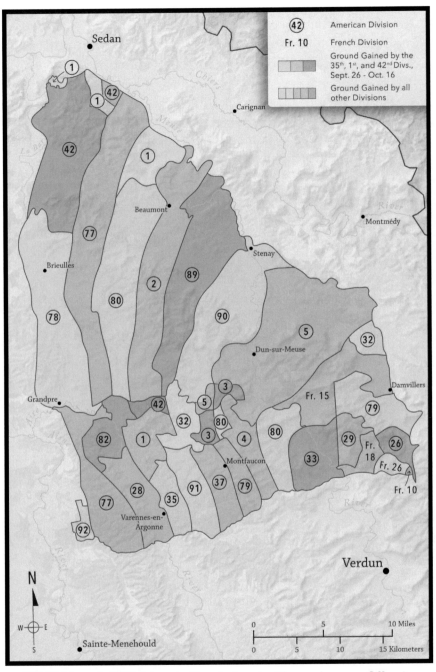

ABMC Map of all Divisions in line during the Meuse-Argonne Offensive

A goal of the Meuse-Argonne offensive was to convince German High Command that its war was lost and it should hurry the peace process.[34] Pershing instructed the 1st Army to move forward "with great vigor."[35] Despite his wishes, that did not happen.[36]

The order opening the battle stated that "the Army was to break through the enemy's successive fortified zones to include the Kriemhilde Stellung, of the Hindenburg Line."[37] The nine American divisions lined up on September 26, 1918, with orders to advance ten miles, which ultimately would require three weeks. The Meuse-Argonne sector's natural defenses contributed to the delay. Its narrow valleys and succession of hills for placing machine guns made it ideal for defensive positions that were deadly to attackers.[38]

The Meuse-Argonne offered some Americans their first action of the war.[39] Despite their lack of experience, they were encouraged by recent successes, and many approached the Argonne battles with confidence. However, they would soon discover they held an inflated sense of American ability.[40]

The Meuse-Argonne's first phase and the 35th Division's failure

Like other Americans, the men of the 35th Division held great confidence as they approached the front.[41] Their division, a National Guard unit from Missouri and Kansas, received partial training at Camp Doniphan, Oklahoma, before going to France in May 1918. Commanded by Maj. Gen. Peter E. Traub, a West Point graduate, it served under the British for two months of easy training in the Vosges Mountains.[42] However, it had not yet faced hard soldiering, and its best preparation for real fighting had been limited patrolling against Germans in a quiet sector of Lorraine.

The division, previously scattered throughout France, came together in the Argonne for what would be its only battle. It relieved the French 73rd Division there on September 21, 1918.[43] The French had tried for years to capture Vauquois, where frequent mine warfare occurred. Maj. Gen. Hunter Liggett, who commanded I Corps and had earned Pershing's trust and respect, had placed the 35th Division on the right of his corps and on the point of the attack.

Of Liggett's three divisions, the 35th was by far the weakest, especially with regard to signals.[44] Its two brigade commanders, brigadier generals, and three of its four regimental commanders, full colonels, had been replaced just prior to battle.[45] Among the division's four regiments (which included the 137th, 138th, 139th, and 140th) only the 140th had served at St. Mihiel, though even it experienced no actual fighting there.[46] Its new leader was formerly the division ordinance officer and had no combat experience. Nonetheless, the 140th Infantry enjoyed the best reputation in the 35th Division and was sometimes touted as an example of the division's usefulness.[47]

On the afternoon of September 22 the 35th Division received its orders and notice that the Meuse-Argonne operation would commence four days later, on September 26.[48]

Day One: Thursday, September 26, 1918

The 35th was ordered to fight through open lands along the Aire River valley, which had excellent brush and trees for concealment. It was to take a series of villages and small towns—Varennes, Cheppy, Véry, Charpentry, Baulny, Exermont, and Fléville—before reaching its distant objective, Hill 260, the Côte de Châtillon.

A few hours before dawn, the moon and the stars appeared in the sky as the soldiers got ready for the jump-off.[49] Morale was high for the 0500 attack. The battle opened with artillery preparation that was to be followed by a rolling barrage in front of infantry. One officer recalled "suddenly feeling young, strong and victorious," adding that "there was little evidence of excitement and none of fear."[50]

The Allies sent up 821 airplanes that morning, 604 of them piloted by Americans and the others by Frenchmen. Compared to the 1,500 airplanes used for St. Mihiel, this was a weaker offensive—a lesser operation. Germans directed many artillery fire missions from airplanes without apparent hindrance from the American air service. Before noon, the Germans, who controlled the air space, had shot down three balloons, which Americans used for observations such as describing the terrain or giving troop coordinates.

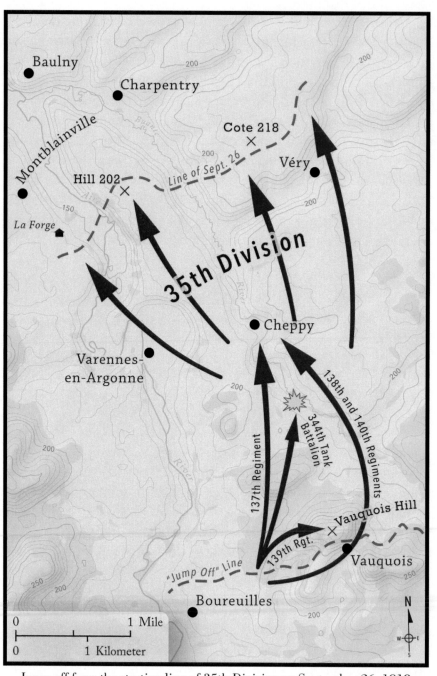

Jump-off from the starting line of 35th Division on September 26, 1918

The US 1st Aero Squadron failed to keep a plane over the 35th Division at all times as ordered. Seven US planes from one squadron flew over the line of advance on the first day, and five were lost.[51] However, the Americans did have some small successes. First Lt. Robert C. Paradise, 12th Aero Squadron, flew low over the lines in the first two hours, and his plane was riddled. He put four hundred rounds of machine gun bullets into enemy positions before destroying a German signal station, which troops used to dispatch communications between various areas.[52]

The Americans, French, and British massed artillery across a twenty-three-mile front, depriving five divisions of their regularly assigned artillery.[53] Nearly 4,000 pieces—2,275 of them American— were echeloned by size. Field Order No. 20 called for mustard and other persistent poison gases to be fired on German artillery positions along the Aire River.[54] American chemical missions fired gases that quickly dissipated, though all gas bombardment was halted four hours before the attack to protect advancing Americans.[55]

A quarter-million rounds of high-explosive artillery shells went out in three hours. With many inexperienced gunners and fire direction centers, much American artillery failed to reach its maximum firepower. Some smaller guns fired randomly. Some machine gun battalions fired barrages blindly into the fog.[56] Many fire missions were plotted inefficiently from maps, without the benefit of ground survey or forward observers to adjust fire.

American and French artillery fired seventy-eight thousand rounds in three days supporting the 35th Division attack, with most of it on the first day. Of that, the 35th Division Artillery put out three thousand rounds in four hours.[57]

Troops were not in trenches at jump-off, so the infantry did not go over the top. They moved forward in a blanket of white fog. It was mobile warfare with artillery and tank support in woods of small trees surrounded by a plain with streams and gullies. The infantry formed in a column of brigades with regiments abreast. Battalions in each regiment were stacked with front units, reserve units, and support units in order. The 344th Tank Battalion led across the front. Many units failed to meet their attack schedules. Visibility in the fog was approximately twenty meters, no more than thirty-five.

Gas and smoke covered Vauquois Hill, which stood about 300 meters long and 120 high in front of the infantry, who were forced to travel by compass.[58] The 137th and 139th regiments went to the left of Vauquois, with the 139th in charge of taking the hill, a formidable site that had blocked the French advance for several years. Though it was defended by well-dug-in German artillery, the Germans had spread their troops along a wide front in face of the Allied attack, leaving the site less defended than previously. Though the Americans had never seen such a well-protected hill, taking it turned out to be a far easier assignment than they expected. While the 137th and the 139th went to the left of Vauquois Hill, the 138th and 140th went to the right. The move was well planned and caught Pershing's attention; he later described it as clever.[59] In an hour Lt. Col. Carl L. Ristine, commanding the 139th Regiment, and his men overran the position and planted American and French flags there, atop the first of the many big hills that must be taken.[60]

Afterward, Ristine's regiment passed through the 137th, only to have enemy machine guns appear to their rear. The melee separated his three battalions, which began picking up casuals (soldiers separated from their units), mostly from the 91st Division and a machine gun battalion.[61]

Americans exhibited many acts of personal heroism that day. William E. Sloan, a 137th Infantry mechanic, while wounded, guided a tank to an enemy machine gun nest and was killed.[62] Capt. Math English, 344th Tank Battalion, dismounted and guided his tank through "three hostile trenches" while under fire near Cheppy.[63] Pvt. Sam Goldberg, Headquarters, 138th Infantry, entered an enemy dugout alone and captured eighteen Germans.[64] Another soldier, Pvt. Edgar H. O'Dell, Company K, 137th Infantry, showed similar courage when he ran into a German building alone, taking four machine guns and sixteen enemy soldiers.[65]

Troops going cross-country had difficulty maintaining direction, but Sgt. Frank J. Kilfoyle, Company M, 139th Infantry, led an automatic rifle squad that killed a German major and members of his machine gun crew.[66] Bugler Charles B. Rymer, with Company F,

138th Infantry, captured a German officer, then, with two other soldiers, killed an enemy soldier, and took twenty-three prisoners.[67] Pvt. Barnard Stone, Company B, 138th Infantry, entered a German dugout alone, killed a German, captured six prisoners and two machine guns, and was wounded twice.[68] Pvt. Birtrus Kemmerer, Company H, 139th Infantry, assisted a wounded officer to safety and was himself wounded.[69]

Some of the most courageous fighting came from the 138th Infantry's Company I, whose commander, Cptn. Alexander R. Skinker, was killed while leading three infantry platoons in front of Cheppy.[70] In the most daring act of the day, Company I's Pvt. Nels Wold, known as the "Big Swede," silenced a machine gun, killed an officer, and took eleven prisoners. While rushing another machine gun, he was killed; he was posthumously awarded a Congressional Medal of Honor.[71] The 138th's Mess Sgt. Herbert S. Taylor volunteered to assist men from another company. Then, alone and under fire, he captured eighteen prisoners.[72] First Lt. Edward H. Price, 138th Infantry, captured a machine gun nest. His company captured four guns and 124 prisoners.[73]

Despite the heroics of many men, some conduct was less favorable. Newly promoted Lt. Col. George S. Patton, age thirty-two, commanded the tank regiment in front of the 35th, and he was particularly disgruntled by witnessing casuals, stragglers, and some officers who lacked competence.

Patton had been brought to France by General Pershing in June 1917 as a staff officer. Patton spent the first few months in France as the adjutant and commandant at Chaumont. Predictably, this job grew tiresome, and he patiently waited for a battlefield command. As the American Expeditionary Forces (AEF) inched closer to fielding an army, his perseverance paid off when Pershing opted to establish a US Army Tank Corps. Volunteers were needed, and Patton jumped at the chance to serve with the new combat arm.

With Pershing's blessing, he became a tank officer in November 1917, and he spent the next several months observing British and French tanks in action, setting up a light-tank training center, and recruiting and organizing tank brigades. He was promoted from captain to major five months before leading the tanks into battle at St. Mihiel.

In the Meuse-Argonne an artillery battery with a platoon of infantry was assigned to protect the tanks.[74] With two-man crews, tanks had no room for a passenger. Disgusted by the apparent cowardice of infantry without officers, Patton followed the tanks into battle on foot and organized a group of infantry casuals, which he led into combat.[75] Five men were killed, and Patton was evacuated on the first day after being wounded in the upper thigh.[76] Though he led the men only briefly, presumably he left an impression, as he later said, "I think I killed one man. He would not work so I hit him on the head with a shovel."[77]

The day helped shape Patton's concept of tank warfare and soldierly behavior, which carried over to his service in WWII. That day, when forty-three tanks were stopped by enemy action and mechanical failure, was Patton's only day of combat and probably the last American tank action of distinction in the war. Of the 189 tanks in the Argonne operation, Americans commanded 142 in the 1st Provisional Tank Regiment; the Germans had no tanks.[78]

Tank on its way to support 35th Division near Varennes, September 26, 1918. Second Lt. Joseph R. Younglove, Company C, 345th Tank Battalion, 304th Tank Brigade, on his way to support the 35th Division near Varennes, September 26, 1918, the day Colonel Patton, commanding the brigade, was injured.

Patton's dissatisfaction with American performance was warranted. Some attack orders were issued by people with little grasp of the front. Some giving orders were in headquarters located far in the rear. The pigeons, available for communication, were usually not used effectively; some refused to fly true due to smoke or the noise of artillery.[79] The initial German reaction to the attack was swift, strong, and easy, facilitated by most of the Americans' inexperience.

Despite many flaws in the US operation and poor performance of many units, the September 26 attack came off with complete secrecy. Division orders said, "Objectives were to be reached on the afternoon of D Day," the day of the attack.[80] But the attack generally stopped when the enemy was met. That was the story of the division throughout the first day, when the enemy evacuated Varennes before noon. As the battle progressed, the Americans took many prisoners, a sign that the German troops' resolve was weakening.[81] The Germans offered no resistance at Cheppy, and hundreds surrendered.[82] Col. Henry J. Reilly, commander of the 149th Field Artillery, would later write in the Rainbow Division history, "There was no more successful surprise during the war than that caused by our First, Fifth and Third Army Corps."[83]

Orders called for infantry to stop moving forward and to hold in place on reaching the first objective, a tactical method held over from Foch's "Limited Objective" plans. In this approach, Foch would attack relentlessly but not over-extend his armies, thereby avoiding heavy losses.[84]

The Americans used smoke for cover as they established a line from Véry to the Aire River east of La Forge. On the first day of the Meuse-Argonne campaign Ligget's I Corps had pushed forward for five miles but was ordered to advance no further. Liggett complained that this stopped the whole machinery of attack, which was difficult to set in motion again. He later recalled losing "six hours during which the enemy was able to bring up reinforcements all along the line. After the attack started there should have been no halt for the Corps except the one imposed by the resistance of the enemy."[85]

The 35th Division advanced to the line Cote 218–Hill 202, nearly three miles on the first day.[86] A post-war study concluded that it maintained the tempo required to conduct effective and sustained offensive operations that day.[87] Despite this, at the end of the day, only the 140th Infantry remained in fighting trim. The 35th Division had become a weak link in the American front.[88]

The 77th Division encountered another kind of problem: its sector's tangled vegetation and German wire left from the 1914 fighting. Even without opposition, one company advanced only two miles on the first day, and at no place did the attackers maintain a single wave of attack. Communication was poor, and once shooting started, stragglers dropped out of the fighting and weakened the line. Despite these imperfections, an official report described the first day as satisfactory, "except in front of Montfaucon."[89] The hill there was still in German hands, and its artillery fire kept raining down on the Americans. The day's advances had been smaller than planned, but by evening the Americans were several miles closer on the road to Germany.[90]

Day Two: Friday, September 27, 1918

A supreme effort was called for on the second day, but confusion reigned. The original jump-off planned for 0530 was changed to 0830 to accommodate artillery. Then the time was changed back to 0530, too late for the artillery to support a then-scheduled 0630 attack. Infantry finally went off at 0930 without any artillery.[91]

Pershing and Traub shared responsibility for the mix-up with the 60th Field Artillery Brigade's commander, Brig. Gen. Lucien Berry. His guns fired only twelve thousand shells into German positions that day, as opposed to forty thousand the day before. Berry faced criticism for not pushing his men and for the slow rates of fire of his guns.[92]

The exhilaration troops felt on the first day was gone.[93] Low ceilings and overcast skies did not stop German airplanes from adjusting artillery. Their airfields were fully developed and in place, having been located there through four years of occupation. Their flyers knew the area and were experienced in navigating with only occasional glimpses of the ground. Furthermore, the American command had miscalculated the challenges the army would face in moving across this terrain. American roads to the front were quagmires, and the mud caused the infantry more problems than German trenches. Vehicles carrying the wounded seriously affected the flow of ammunition and supplies to the front. Horses and mules were so scarce that men sometimes pushed machine gun and food carts. Though those problems were substantial enough, the American delays also allowed Germany time to bring in reinforcements. [94]

September 27, day two of the attack, saw little firing of Allied artillery. Tanks came up but did not fight. Inexperienced soldiers were often under little or no control and moved in groups and clumps rather than organized formations. They exercised little march discipline, and probably only a few understood that the division was coming apart. Some commanders did not command, and others went to the extreme of trying to control every man in every squad. After the first day there was no telephone wire in place, so all communication consisted of hand-carried messages.

Battery C, 120th Field Artillery with short "Schneiders," Varennes, September 27, 1918.

Units struggled to maintain leadership as officers incurred wounds. The 137th Infantry's lieutenant colonel was wounded and evacuated. On the previous day the regiment's colonel, a man well advanced in years, had been exhausted and evacuated. [95] The captain leading the point battalion of the mixed regiments was wounded, leaving the battalion with only one captain. The sergeant major and battalion interpreter were killed.

Many soldiers displayed extraordinary courage in the face of such casualties. Sgt. Willie A. Oldfield, Company I, 139th Infantry, led a charge against machine guns that were delaying the troops from reaching Charpentry.[96] Sgt. Hearl Smith, Company F, 140th, wounded during an assault on a machine gun nest, continued to lead his half-platoon until he died from his injuries.[97]

The 139th Infantry attacked at noon with tank support and advanced 300 meters. The 140th attempted to resume its own advance at 1400 but failed. At 1730 it launched a second attack after securing additional tank and artillery support and dug in northeast of Chaudron Farm, a German-occupied farmhouse, after a total advance of five miles in two days.[98] The 137th and 139th advanced at 1800 and took the villages of Charpentry and Baulny.

The brigade commander then ordered the 138th and 140th Infantry Regiments to retreat for the night to the positions they held the previous evening. In the process, some men started to run to the rear in panic. About three hundred were stopped and turned back. Everything then became quiet and held. The 140th's 2nd and 3rd Battalions dug in for the night on a ridge northeast of Charpentry.[99]

One of Traub's biggest successes was in stopping the rout of those men near Charpentry, but it came at great cost. The amount of land captured and held on the second day was not as great as on the first day.[100]

That night scouts attempted to locate the enemy and one of the battalions of the 140th that was lost track of during the drive that afternoon. The enemy was not found, though the missing unit was nearby. At 2300 I Corps directed the assault be resumed at 0530.[101] Despite the 35th Division's capture of Charpentry and the 79th Division's capture of Montfaucon on the Giselher Stellung, Pershing was very disappointed by the lack of progress on September 27.

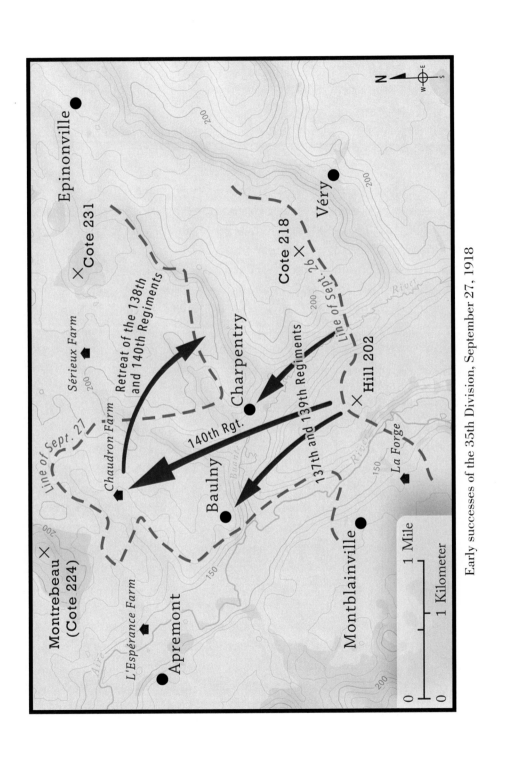

Early successes of the 35th Division, September 27, 1918

Day Three: Saturday, September 28, 1918

The division exhibited some semblance of order at dawn on September 28, but even this outline of organization did not last long. Col. Channing E. "Dogface" Delaplane, the division's only regimental commander able to hold his regiment together, had good control of the 140th as it moved forward at 0530, but it had only one of its three battalions.[102] Delaplane and his men faced other problems as well. The regiment was on the far-right flank in the division advance and caught incoming fire on both flanks. The 91st Division was scheduled to be on the 140th's right but failed to arrive, creating a four-kilometer gap when the 35th Division designated Exermont as the decisive point to take.[103] Twenty tanks reported to the 140th Infantry at 0945, and the left battalion of the regiment's advance was ordered to follow them at three hundred yards. Rather than working in formation as separate units, the 137th and 139th Regiments were badly mixed and had new commanders when beginning their attacks.

Throughout the day, much depended on individual initiatives. Cpl. Thomas E. Wilder of the 137th Infantry's Company F was wounded and continued in combat until he was killed.[104] Cpl. Paul Jeffords, Company A, 137th Infantry, while wounded, took a position behind his squad and directed it from there until he died from the wounds.[105] Sgt. Victor Seagraves, a 1st Battalion Scout who was also of the 139th Infantry, organized a patrol that shot up a German machine gun nest and was killed while advancing on another.[106] Sgt. William R. Myers, Medical Detachment, 137th Infantry, was wounded near the start of the day by a machine gun bullet, but he continued to administer aid to others until he received additional wounds from a shell fragment.[107] After distinguishing himself scouting machine gun positions the previous day, 1st Lt. Clement P. Dickinson, of the 129th Machine Gun Battalion, was killed scouting more positions.[108]

While leading the 140th's attack, the 1st Battalion suffered high casualties. German machine gun nests filled the woods, forcing an intense fight. Only a few American artillery shells were heard going towards enemy lines, and the fighting was so fierce that 3rd Battalion lost most of its officers and half its men. Sgt. Clarence Dry of Company I, 140th Infantry, volunteered to locate a German machine gun nest and was killed.[109] The 3rd Battalion's Company M fought on without officers. Lt. Col. Fred L. Lemmon suffered a serious chest wound, but he "remained in command of his battalion for twenty-four hours," leading it under fire and "refusing to be evacuated until he was helpless from loss of blood."[110] He and other Americans demonstrated courage in their attempts to maintain the battle schedule.[111]

Despite such heroics, on this day the division lost the tempo to sustain the attack.[112] No American planes flew above, but enemy planes strafed troops and assisted in adjusting German artillery, providing information on American troop locations so the Germans could target them more accurately. The German high command ordered in reserves once they realized the attack was not a feint, but the Americans' forward motion was stopped in some instances even before German reinforcements arrived.[113] The bulk of those reinforcements appeared when Americans reached the German main line of resistance on September 28.[114]

Division headquarters transmitted instructions for the advance to brigade commanders verbally and by radio. The 35th Division at no time issued formal field orders, and command decisions were improvised on the spot. Its four regiments were formed into two provisional brigades.[115] The Americans set up a division PC (Post of Command) at Cheppy, but Traub did not stay there, and his headquarters was unable to communicate with either of its brigades. Roads were so bad that it was hard to get a motorcycle through. All liaison was poor, and control nearly collapsed.[116]

I Corps had reinforced the 35th Division with an 82nd Division regiment and sent Col. Jens Bugge to act as the 35th Division's Chief of Staff with orders to get some punch into it.[117] Pershing came into 35th Division headquarters that afternoon and said an attack was necessary, asking Bugge what he thought. The colonel said it could not be done then with an assurance of success. Pershing then said, "Well, make it tomorrow morning regardless of cost."[118]

In a departure from standard practice, at 1515 the brigade

commanders left their command posts to lead their infantry regiments from the front, hoping to make the regiments more effective. At 1535 an attempt was made to reorganize the brigades in order to attack at 1730.[119] Portions of the 140th started forward at 1800 and reached Chaudron Farm, the high point of the regiment's advance, two-thirds of a mile to the southeast of Montrebeau Wood. Attacking at about the same time as the 140th, elements of the 139th Infantry reached Chaudron Farm at 1900. Maj. John Henry O'Connor of the 137th Infantry led an attack on Montrebeau Wood and held the northern edge that night with elements of two other regiments, the 138th and 139th.[120]

Some gains were made on September 28, and at one point, Charpentry, Baulny, and Chaudron Farm were all in American hands. The 35th Division captured Montrebeau Wood and reached a line running from one kilometer northeast of Chaudron Farm to l'Espérance Farm. The successful attack carried the front line of the division into and to the east of Montrebeau Wood.[121] However, most gains were later lost throughout the day as the 35th and the 1st Army's other eight divisions struggled to hold—and in some cases even to gain—ground.

Overall, it was clear that the opening phase of the big 1st Army campaign had failed.[122] Pershing had set unrealistic expectations for his inexperienced doughboys and thought that somehow, they would have by now crossed the main German defensive line. Only one key objective, Montfaucon, remained in American hands. The Germans completely halted the American advance on the third day of the Meuse-Argonne offensive, and from then on, the fighting would be desperate, with every foot fiercely contested by the Germans.[123]

Day Four: Sunday, September 29, 1918

Pershing ordered Traub to attack again on the morning of September 29, and Traub passed the order to the regiments.[124] At 0534 125 men from the 137th Infantry jumped off from the northern edge of Montrebeau Wood.[125] By 0610 they were enveloped by heavy fire immediately south of Exermont, and they withdrew at about 0800.[126]

At 0630 the 140th started forward again in a column of battalions

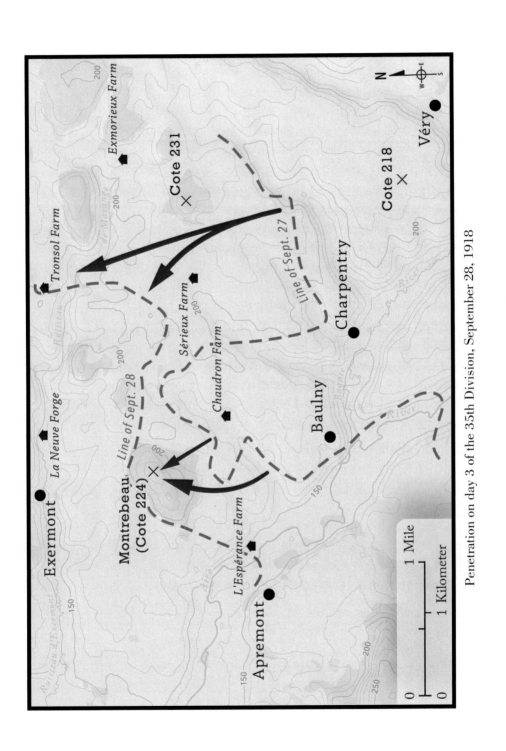

Penetration on day 3 of the 35th Division, September 28, 1918

toward Exermont and Bois de Boyon. Again, there was no artillery barrage for the infantry to follow, but between 0800 and 1000 the attack succeeded in capturing the Beauregard Farm and the Neuville-le-Comte Farm north of Exermont Creek. The battalions dug in there, and Traub came up to investigate. He ordered a withdrawal after recognizing the German strength and American weakness at the position, largely due to the losses the regiment had suffered.[127] Around 1100 he sent the following message to Liggett at I Corps: "Can't advance beyond crest south of Exermont, thoroughly disorganized. Request that we be replaced with fresh troops."[128]

That afternoon a German counterattack north of Exermont Creek reached the southern edge of Montrebeau Wood, and the 35th withdrew to the ridge northeast of Baulny. It held the position that night and strengthened it the next morning, repulsing all enemy attempts after that. The Germans made feints at the outpost line during the day, but they did nothing of consequence. At night, the 35th faced incoming German artillery fire and poison gas.[129]

Some soldiers in the 35th had exhibited bravery during the day's events. For example, Maj. Parker C. Kalloch, 137th Infantry, while wounded, organized and led an attack.[130] However, the heroics of individual men were ultimately not enough to keep the division's efforts afloat.

Between September 26-29, the 140th endured four days of heavy enemy fire with no American artillery support, and its manpower diminished from 3,700 to 1,200. No record of losses by day is available.[131] Throughout this period, many officers also died, causing rapid shifts in command. Major Davis of 3rd Battalion was killed at about the same time as Col. H. W. Parker, commanding the 138th Infantry.[132] Command of the 140th Infantry Regiment passed to a captain. In most units, legally issued orders were not being carried out, because some brigade and regimental commanders did not know what to do next. Some completely lost control, and their commands became ineffective as combat forces.[133] Next to Pershing, Traub bore responsibility for that situation. His command skills "could not be described as much better than posturing, hanging

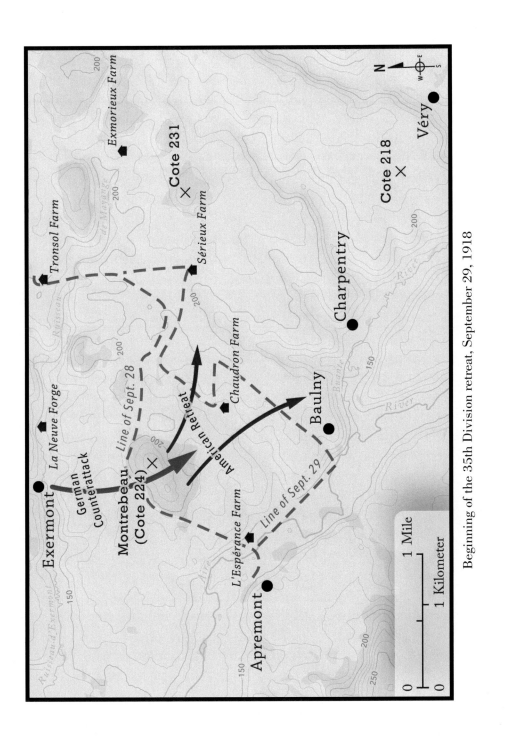

Beginning of the 35th Division retreat, September 29, 1918

back, remaining remote, showing himself here and there, and then impulsively taking actions."[134]

In addition to the leadership issues, the Americans faced challenges of strength. Their local attacks met limited success, as the Germans always counterattacked, sometimes driving back American units that had originally succeeded. As in most combat situations, nothing worked as planned.[135]

On the fourth day of attack, Pershing called a three-day halt. He was virtually incapable of doing more, as some of the original attack divisions had been sent reeling by German counterattacks. Facing rough terrain, determined resistance, and heavy German artillery, the 35th was badly beaten. For the first time in the war, American divisions were forced to retreat. On the night of September 29-30, 1918, Pershing ordered it replaced with the 1st Division.[136] As it retreated, the 35th Division Infantry was followed by its artillery, depriving the replacement division of 72 guns that would have dramatically increased its firepower.[137]

Pershing also pulled other attacking divisions from the front, including the 91st, 37th, and 79th to the 35th's right. They were all green, but the 1st US Army viewed the 35th as the biggest failure of the four divisions. An inspector deplored its lack of discipline, citing the way company grade officers (captains and lower) gave little or no attention to saluting and fraternized with the men while field grade officers looked on with indifference. He said the division had a "National Guard mentality," reflecting a common belief that National Guard units did not receive adequately rigorous training.[138]

The 35th Division, having made the farthest advances on its first day and succeeding in briefly getting into part of Exermont on September 29, simply fell apart.[139] Its flanks were out of touch with its adjoining divisions. Many of its units were commingled or out of touch with each other. Maj. Gen. Robert Lee Bullard, who knew all the divisions, wrote, "The 35th Division was thrice cursed… It was infested by politicians… Some of its Regular officers were of poor quality, and some of its Guard leaders were appointees with pull, untrained and incompetent."[140]

Although the 35th had advanced more than six miles since

September 26, it paid a terrible toll for the ground it captured, then lost. When it was pulled from the line, the division had suffered more than six thousand casualties, and nearly half its infantry was dead or hospitalized. The other half was overcome from fatigue.[141] No other 1st Army division had so many casualties this early in the battle. The time had come for combat-ready and experienced troops to take the lead.

In the end, the officers and men of the 35th Division failed to recognize just how much they were out of order or the extent of their failure. Its problems ran much deeper than poor saluting and lack of march discipline. Severe criticism of the division came as a shock, and they resented it. Though the division's officers and men tended to blame the Regular Army for not having trained and led them better, three congressional inquiries eventually investigated the unit's breakdown.

Cptn. Harry S. Truman, who was to become the thirty-third President of the United States, commanded Battery D, 129th Field Artillery of the 35th Division. He described some of his experiences in a letter to his future wife Bess, "The great drive has taken place. . . . The experience has been one that I don't want to go through again . . . but I'd never have missed it for anything. I shot out a German battery, shot up his big Observation Post and ruined another battery when it was moving down the road."[142] Truman defended the division during the war and much later while in the White House. The officers and men of the artillery battery that he commanded in the Meuse-Argonne marched in his inaugural parade.

Prior to the attack Pershing called the 35th "the best-looking lot of men I have in France."[143] Afterward he was sympathetic toward Traub's men and refused to openly criticize their battlefield performance, stating, "The 35th suffered greater casualties than any other division during those first four days of continuous fighting."[144] The fact is the Kansas-Missouri troops and other AEF doughboys failed early in Meuse-Argonne because of the poor performance of inexperienced and poorly trained soldiers and leaders. Their defeat shocked all ranks, but the Germans were better trained and better tacticians.

The problems were not isolated to the 35th Division, however. Mere days into battle the 1st Army struggled to advance, while its casualties mounted and worsened as German resistance stiffened after Gallwitz brought up additional reserves. Clogged roads, poor weather, and the next wave of the influenza pandemic compounded the enemy fire.

Pershing saw no choice but to stop the attack and regroup for a few days. After the American retreat—with the 1st US Army now seventeen days behind its schedule—Pershing devoted more men to the attack and started conducting frontal assaults on a wide front that ultimately involved twenty-nine American and four French divisions.[145]

Though other divisions battled on, for the most part the war had ended for Traub and the 35th Division. After some rest, the doughboys from Kansas and Missouri were placed in a quiet sector as a reserve division and remained there until the Armistice.

CHAPTER 2

The 1st Division in the Argonne

A new battle

The first few days of the Meuse-Argonne campaign had proven that the Americans would not have an easy victory. After being stopped by the Germans, a less determined leader might have called it a failure and ended the campaign. Instead, General Pershing hoped to regain momentum by placing his best three Regular Army divisions on the point in each corps.[146]

Pershing replaced three divisions and moved a fourth to another location, immediately shifting a total of 125,000 men.[147] This time he brought only experienced soldiers into the fighting: the 1st Division (Regular Army), the 3rd Division (Regular Army) and the 32nd Division (National Guard). The new order of battle was the 33rd, 4th, 80th, 3rd, 32nd, 1st, 28th, and 77th Divisions, left to right. The US Divisions were in the I, V, and III Corps, all of which were to be rearranged in the course of the Argonne battles. The 1st US Army outnumbered the five German divisions in the sector.[148]

Pershing ordered two of his best divisions, the 1st and the 32nd, into the line on the night of September 30.[149] The 1st was assigned to I Corps, commanded by the trusted Gen. Liggett. The 32nd, a good National Guard unit from Michigan and Wisconsin with many German speakers, was assigned to V Corps. Both divisions were ordered to attack the distant Heights of Romagne, which encompassed the most dominant positions from which the Germans defended the Hindenburg Line. The 1st was to take the Côte de Châtillon, and the 32nd was to take Côte Dame Marie, both German defensive positions that could provide support to each other as part of the Hindenburg Line.

Maj. Gen. Charles G. Summerall, an artillery expert who had

commanded the 1st Division since July 1918, enjoyed a reputation for bloodshed.[150] He was known for transferring officers to Blois, a town in the Loire Valley that served as a zone in the rear of the battle, with little thought. Every soldier joked about officers being sent to "Bluey," an expression that acknowledged the letdown or depression that followed being sent to Blois, which typically happened when men had failed and would be reassigned.[151]

Summerall did not believe the poor German defense of St. Mihiel represented the real quality of the German Army. He believed the Germans defending the Argonne would be tougher as they fought for their homeland, and the 35th Division's experience verified his instincts.[152]

As he prepared to replace the 35th, Summerall also knew that the Meuse-Argonne posed particularly formidable natural challenges. In time of peace the area was a large, wild forest of beech, oak, fir, and birch trees. It had ravines filled with brush and some open land.[153] The Germans had capitalized on this landscape, compounding its dangers. Martin Hogan, a member of the 42nd Division, later described the area: "The [Argonne] forest itself was a natural obstacle of greatest difficulty, a wilderness of rough country cut with narrow valleys, twisting gullies, sharp, unexpected hills, nasty hollows, and always choked with heavy tree and underbrush growth. Moreover, the Germans had worked upon the defenses of this natural entanglement from the early days of the war, multiplying Nature's pitfalls a hundred times, strewing the whole with devil machines and hidden mines, and weaving the toughest thickets with thousands of yards of barbed wire, thus making every natural obstacle into a small fortress."[154]

The troops were to confront these German defenses as they advanced. Despite being in different corps, the divisions were ordered to move alongside each other in the advance. Each was to go as far as possible as quickly as possible, pushing straight ahead without regard to flanks. It was mostly open field, mobile warfare over hills and valleys until they reached the Kriemhilde Stellung, the area where four lines came together in a zone of elaborate trenches that did not exist elsewhere in the sector. Named for the Wagnerian witch associated with revenge, this position defended the double-track German railroad from Metz, part of the entire German supply system.[155] Because it moved troops and freight, the railroad served as an indispensable resource to the German military efforts.

Summerall knew the Kriemhilde Stellung would be fiercely defended. Though most German soldiers suffered from poor morale, their first-class divisions of infantry and machine guns, with excellent artillery backing, continued to show tactical efficiency and individual courage. The original German line, which stretched across occupied western France from the English Channel to Switzerland, remained in place—further proof of the German resolve.

Still, Summerall and his men had advantages the 35th Division lacked. Most of the original 1st Division soldiers were well trained, with service on the Mexican Border in 1916-1917. Furthermore, it was the most combat-experienced American division in France. Both Allies and Germans respected it for taking Cantigny and holding it against two counterattacks. That battle, which occurred on May 28, 1918, and in which the 1st Division lost over five thousand men, was the first successful US operation and therefore the first to demonstrate that Americans could actually defeat Germans.

Still, the division faced some detractors. Many of its newly enlisted replacements and draftees had farming or laboring backgrounds, and some were immigrants. Some were recent arrivals from the Austro-Hungarian and Russian Empires or descended from Central, Eastern, and Southern European immigrants. A German officer called them "semi-Americans," but in actuality they were proud to serve and became some of the army's best men.[156]

However, the men did not make the greatest first impression off the battlefield. Capt. George C. Marshall, after meeting the 1st Division upon its arrival to France, commented on how little impressed he was by its personnel, noting, "Many of the men were undersized and a number spoke English with difficulty."[157] Henry Russell Miller echoed this sentiment in a 1920 division history that noted his first impression of the unit: "It did not look heroic. Physically it was less impressive than any outfit I have ever seen. In intelligence it was probably a little below the American average, in education certainly. It spoke a dozen tongues."[158]

Despite its men's initial appearance, the division's Regular Army culture changed ordinary soldiers into a real fighting team. It set an extreme standard of discipline in which no one questioned taking orders or observing military courtesy to the highest standard. This discipline, which became a way of life, was especially important because of the division's high number of casualties. The substantial losses, including five thousand at Cantigny and nearly seven thousand at Soissons, required the survivors' toughness and culture to quickly rub off on replacements.

The army had no fully formed infantry divisions when the United States entered the war. The 1st Division was essentially created by "cherry picking" the men from existing Regular Army units, such as the 41st Division. It received preference in the quality and number of replacements. Cpl. Earl R. Poorbaugh, a WWI veteran of the division, served as a correspondent in World War II and remembered that his "1st Division officers in 1917–1918 were 100% superior, all were strict but fair. It contained a solid core of officers and men from Regular Army units."[159]

The demands of war created many opportunities for both officers and enlisted men to receive promotions. Many of the enlisted were experienced "Old Army" veterans from the Philippines and Mexico. They usually lacked substantial education but were capable, disciplined, and experienced low-level leaders who knew how to give and take orders. Common soldiers and mustangs (officers newly promoted from enlisted ranks) were treated with respect. Expert riflemen earned a $5.00 premium every payday. Many experienced company clerks received the opportunity to apply for direct commissions. Unique skills counted, and an enlisted man with no knowledge of French before reaching the country learned it quickly enough to become an interpreter. It was not uncommon for soldiers to replace officers wounded or killed in combat. Education or background had nothing to do with it; the enlisted men who advanced were most likely to be good fighters.

Practically all infantry battalion and machine gun battalion commanders had been in France for a year. No favoritism was shown to the old hands, who purchased cigarettes at the YMCA at standard prices just like everybody else. The division worked hard to achieve a professional culture and set a good example for new soldiers.[160]

By the time of the Argonne, the 1st Division was experienced in operations in France, with more combat time than any unit in the AEF.[161] It was also the first American WWI division to have combat experience in both offensive and defensive operations. At the time of the Argonne fighting, all rifle companies were led by experienced captains, most of whom had commanded their units for at least a year. Approximately one-fourth of enlisted men were veterans of battles other than St. Mihiel, and all had participated in that operation. While the division had little hard combat at St. Mihiel and suffered only light casualties there, it gained valuable experience in leap-frogging and passing through companies and battalions during the attack. This practice built great teamwork.

Moving to the front

On September 27 most of the 1st Division started moving to the new front by forced marches beginning at 1300. One officer, Lyman S. Frasier, said it was "never to be forgotten."[162] During a halt some of the officers and men wounded at Soissons rejoined their old units and received a warm welcome.[163] That night the remainder of the division fell out, formed a line, and headed into the woods just south of Verdun, marching all night to a bivouac. When they discovered it was surrounded by anti-aircraft guns manned by badly crippled veterans of the French Army, the Americans were impressed.

There was only one way to the front, and it was the same access road used by all of I Corps. It was sometimes filled with stalled vehicles, a situation that worsened when Germans blew a forty-foot hole in the crude plank affair.[164] Navigating the distance, the natural terrain, and the man-made obstacles required substantial stamina, and the men marched to near-exhaustion. Pvt. Herbert B. McHenry wrote of arriving in a forest just before dawn, describing how he and his unit "broke ranks, fell out, placed [their] blankets on the ground and went to sleep without taking off [their] shoes."[165]

Engineers with wire cutters led the troops cross-country by

compass to Nixéville, a convenient spot on the way to their objective. Every rifleman carried a pack, blanket, gas mask, personal weapon, basic load of ammunition, and half a pup tent. Soldiers tugged and pulled each other through ditches and over obstacles. Machine gunners disassembled their new weapons to carry them. Weighing fifty-three pounds, the French Hotchkiss machine guns were divided, and individual machine gunners carried 250 rounds of ammunition. Every man carried part of the total load.

Though the men understood the danger they were approaching, they found new evidence of it during their march. While heading to the front, for example, the 26th Infantry discovered seventy 35th Division wounded soldiers abandoned in a church.[166] Such discoveries served as implicit—albeit perhaps unnecessary— reminders of the perils of war.

The 1st Division practiced great caution during the march, and Standing Operating Procedures controlled every aspect of their lives. Foxholes were camouflaged when bivouacking, especially during the day. No fires were allowed to temper the night's darkness. Everybody was to feed and care for the mules as well as possible.[167] They were a priority, as they facilitated transport during the march. Some guns were pulled by trucks, but horses and mules brought up some ammunition.[168] Still, fodder was scarce, and getting the animals fed and groomed was a serious matter.[169] Few horses or mules were to be watered at a time, and lookouts had to watch for airplanes at watering places. Animals were moved to the rear during fighting and were concealed by day.

During the twelve-hour advance in heavy rain, the company commanders led columns of two abreast, with platoon leaders taking up the rear.[170] Getting to the front was slowed and made difficult by streams without bridges, old bivouacs, abandoned "horse lines,"[171] wire entanglements, and trench lines left from four years of German occupation. The division took its first casualties while crossing an old unmarked mine field.

On this move, the soldiers did not maintain the regulation five paces of separation between men in the approach-march formations. Troops were to be in fighting positions by 0300 on September 30, so nervous leaders, whose greatest concern was being late for battle, ignored the soldiers bunching up and pushed for a faster advance.[172] Though the kitchens and some other support units were delayed on the way up, the 1st Division relieved the 35th as scheduled.

The 16th, 18th, 26th, and 28th Infantry Regiments made it into the line on the night of September 30-October 1, and the Engineers with the column moved into positions the next night. Many, but not all, the 1st Division Artillery's 108 guns reached Cheppy that night with the infantry. The 6th Field Artillery Brigade supported the 1st Brigade, and the 7th Field Artillery Brigade supported the 2nd Brigade from concealed positions.[173] The 1st Field Artillery Brigade, the support, was initially unable to get beyond Cheppy but made it to the front the next night. The successful march to the front would be remembered in the division's history as a "remarkable achievement."[174]

Standing procedure was for the unit being replaced to control the operation, since it was engaged with the enemy at the time of replacement. However, no one, including the departing 35th, had any idea where the Germans were.[175] Contrary to established army practice, the 1st Division had priority over the disorganized 35th in all matters of changeover. They decided which weapons and equipment to leave with the 35th Division's outgoing units.[176] German gas and artillery came in while men were spreading out to sleep, a clear reminder of the challenges to come.

Days Five through Eight: September 30 and October 1–3, 1918

By September 30, when the 1st Division reached the front, the Germans had begun to perceive the Americans as weak. Captured German documents said, "According to statements of prisoners, the enemy relaxes on account of the high losses (up to 80%) and complete exhaustion of the 35th American Infantry Division."[177] However, the German Army did not rest in its assumption; it brought six divisions into the Argonne.

The fresh 1st Division troops expected to be committed to combat as soon as they reached the battle line on September 30, but they faced a delay of three days, as the newly reorganized 1st US Army would not be ready to launch an attack across the front until October 4.[178] From the beginning of the wait, every man constantly risked being fired on. Even a lone soldier could draw indirect artillery fire and flat trajectory fire from the three-hundred-foot ridges of the Argonne plateau overlooking them from the west. The plateau, which looked down on the American avenue of approach along the Aire River and the Aire River Valley, provided the Germans many fine artillery positions. The Germans would not stop using that ridge for an artillery base until it was taken from them by force. [179]

Traffic jam in Cheppy, October 1, 1918.

After arriving the 1st Division started preparing for the imminent attack. Two hospitals and 1st Division Headquarters were set up in Cheppy on September 30. 1st Brigade, consisting of the 16th and 18th Infantry Regiments, also set up a Post of Command (PC) there, while the 2nd Brigade, with its 26th and 28th Infantry Regiments, set up at Charpentry.[180] Despite the preparation, the surroundings remained somber. Shell holes and splintered trees cluttered the landscape. Soupy roads were so bad they could hardly be seen, and no bridges remained. Nine German planes flew over the 1st Division before dusk on September 30, and US troops brought down two enemy balloons heavily defended by airplanes and anti-aircraft guns.[181]

Summerall wrote his attack order on October 1, the first day in the division's new position. However, he waited to issue it, planning to turn the 1st Division's part in the general offensive into a series of smaller set-piece battles.[182] First, he placed the 1st Battalion of the 16th Infantry, about eight hundred men, in reserve "to be preserved for some unexpected, yet decisive need."[183] He also earmarked the regiment's Machine Gun Company, with about two hundred men, for the elite force that would accomplish this yet-to-be-determined mission.

Setting aside a large infantry unit with a machine gun battalion was not the usual way of doing things, but Summerall determined to keep these thousand men out of the battle until "he saw fit to divide the attack of the 1st Division into three phases; one dealing with the 1st Brigade, one with the 2nd Brigade and one with the 1st Battalion of the 16th Infantry Regiment."[184]

As the division prepared for battle it spread out over a thousand-yard front with all four infantry regiments side by side in the Exermont Ravine, the main ravine from which others branched.[185] Leading battalions were put in place along the ravine directly in front of Cote 240. Support battalions were in the second ravine, and reserve battalions in the next, the Véry Ravine.[186] Most companies were led by captains with enough combat experience to qualify them for promotion to battalion commanders (majors) while on the job. Still, there were many dead horses, mules, and people on the battlefield. All of the artillerymen, who would provide the barrage to help prepare the terrain for their advancing fellow soldiers, knew a supreme test was ahead.[187]

Machine gun companies were assigned to specific infantry battalions so they could identify with each other as part of a team. It was important for the automatic weapons gunners and riflemen to know each other, because it fostered camaraderie. Each lived and ate with its assigned infantry.[188]

Though crucial during battle, machine gun companies held little value during the delay. From October 1 to October 3 the sector was perfect hell for the 1st Division. German snipers continually shot at everyone, testing morale.[189] Enemy artillery high explosive (HE) fire, which detonates with great velocity, mixed with gas rounds coming from German positions high in the Argonne. Casualties were heavy, and over the three days, the 1st Division accumulated 1,660 casualties (wounded, gassed, and killed), roughly 10 percent of the its infantry.[190]

Germans drenched the ravines and low places with gas, causing most of the casualties. Gas was a very effective weapon for the Germans, as just a few German gas shells caused more casualties than eight or ten HE rounds. Liquid gas fired by Germans during the night would evaporate in the morning sunshine. Many suffered chemical burns from the gas residual, including the 37th mm gun section of the 18th Infantry Headquarters.[191] According to James Scott Wheeler's history of the 1st Division, one battalion reported 392 mustard gas casualties. The 18th Infantry evacuated more than two hundred effectives, or simple soldiers, to the rear before the gas alarm could be spread and the gassed areas avoided. The Germans fired 3,470 rounds of mustard gas and phosgene—a colorless gas with an odor like musty hay—in small amounts spaced over time during this waiting period.[192]

The Americans resisted using gas for a number of reasons. For starters, using it was against international law. However, they also understood the practical realities of employing gas: first, because gas was subject to the whims of the wind, it could get blown back into Americans' faces, and second, many Americans feared that using gas would result in retaliation.

On October 2 an order from corps instructed the division to send out patrols to make contact, probe enemy defenses, and identify targets for artillery.[193] Two 1st Battalion platoons, consisting of twelve squads from the 26th Infantry's Company A, left before dawn in heavy fog. Many soldiers were hit by shellfire while going into position. Legge later reported that the group "deployed in two waves, the first as skirmishers, the second as squads in files, called squad columns, positioned fifty feet to the rear. The entire body came under heavy fire from three sides, and it was almost wiped out. The patrol of two officers and 77 men withdrew that night with 20 men . . . all but one officer and 13 men were killed or wounded, none captured."[194] During the ill-fated patrol, leader Lt. Thomas D. Amory took three men with him to knock out machine guns. After capturing one nest and killing its crew, he was killed by another shooting from a house nearby. His last words were, "We will take that nest or die trying."[195]

Pvt. Mont R. Keith was a volunteer member of Amory's initial patrol, which succeeded in getting quite close to the enemy. However, such proximity carried a cost, as the men ended up "cut off from their own troops without food and water for thirty-six hours under constant enemy fire." Keith returned to his battalion commander and gave a report before going back to the lost men and guiding them to friendly lines.[196]

During the delay, many soldiers risked their lives, assuming leadership, rescuing comrades, and exhibiting bravery. Sgt. George C. Jackson, Company M, 16th Infantry, reorganized his scattered company and captured German machine guns. Borrowing an automatic rifle, "he advanced on an enemy machine-gun, killing two members of the crew and capturing another."[197] While under fire, Pvt. Austin Gates and three others from the 16th Infantry rescued a wounded soldier outside American-held territory.[198] On October 3, a rescue party led by Pvt. William Howard rescued a wounded comrade, traveling four hundred yards beyond the American position in broad daylight to reach him.[199] On the same day, Pvt. Everett A. Kilmer volunteered to lead a patrol to rescue a wounded rifleman.[200]

Others were eager to lead patrols and rendered invaluable service during the wait. Sgt. Martin Ferentchak, born in Austria, assumed command of a reconnaissance patrol after the leader was killed. He advanced in front of the lines to locate the enemy, where he located and recorded their positions, providing useful intelligence for the October 4 attack.[201] Cpl. Orvel H. Halley, 28th Infantry, led two squads on a similar patrol.[202] Then 1st Lt. Thomas J. Grayson led a patrol into enemy lines and stayed hidden there for thirty-six hours, observing and gathering intelligence. [203]

Germans continued to fire big guns into 1st Division positions, and soldiers distinguished them by sound. Incoming HE rounds made a brief "swish" sound before impact and a flat, dull "thump" noise on impact. Large, flat trajectory rounds screamed for a split second before one heard them. Hostile airplanes flew overhead to spot targets for their artillery. Sometimes German planes would dive on 1st Division machine gun positions. The soldiers could do nothing but sit and take it while waiting for the army-wide attack to begin.

Even while everybody was dug in and taking casualties in a dangerous situation, the leaders tried to keep conditions and discipline close to that of garrison life. Soldiers were required to exercise nightly, shave daily, and wash. [204] They exercised in silence, usually double-timing in place or performing deep knee bends or push-ups. It took careful organizing to get everyone fed without having them under fire. Well-dispersed men received a hot meal at dusk and another between 0200 and 0300. Small groups drifted back to be served in the dark. Kitchens were in the rear, and regimental officers often visited them looking for volunteers to replace wounded infantrymen. [205]

Maintaining fresh drinking water proved challenging. There were no Lister Bags, the large canvas bags that hung on a tripod or from a tree and served as the usual water source for a company-sized body of soldiers in the field. Instead, some men used streams as a source of drinking water, courting dysentery. When water carts were unavailable, groups of soldiers might seek potable water at a watering point in the rear. In these trips, two men carried twenty canteens attached to a pole.

Congested traffic at crater hole near Neuvilly, October 3, 1918.

The division spread out on the south side of the Exermont Ravine. On the north stood rows of buttress-like hills, mostly with woods on top and scrub on the sides. In the modern era the hills are covered with large trees, many of which grew from stumps of trees shattered by war.[206] The most imposing hill, closest to the Exermont Ravine on the north, Hill 240, is sometimes called Côte de Montrefagne or Cote 240, based on its metric height. To the side and somewhat in front of it lay Cotes 212, 269, and 272; beyond that were Cotes 288 and 263. All were German-occupied, provided natural defenses, and offered useful offensive positions, as Germans could direct fire from any of them to the right or left into the flanks of units attacking the other hills.

The large grouping of hills facing the 1st Division was about three miles wide and three miles deep, holding key German positions in front of the 1st US Army. The Americans' mission was to drive a wedge into the hills, which stood scattered in checkerboard fashion throughout the area. This German line of defense seemed endless. When the front-most German position fell, the next hill became the first line of defense. The Americans knew they had to take all these hills before any successful assault could be made on the Côte de Châtillon.[207]

Rumors of peace added to the uncertainty of the interval before the attack. Some rumors were true, and some even became public knowledge. Maj. Freiherr von der Bussche, representing Field Marshall Paul von Hindenburg and Gen. Erich Ludendorff, made a statement on October 2 before the German Parliament, explaining that while it was still possible for the German Army to carry on and inflict losses, Germany could not win the war. On October 3, Hindenburg wrote a statement that it was from now on impossible for Germany to win the peace by force of arms.[208]

The 1st Division never experienced a more trying time than while waiting to jump off on that attack. All 1st Division communication broke down, as shelling had destroyed communications systems, and the Signal Corps lacked sufficient time for repairs. The division took about five hundred casualties a day, so many that it discontinued burial parties.[209] The division did not know the location of the German main line.[210] Meanwhile, the German Army used the four-day interval to strengthen its positions and prepare for the looming attack.[211]

Day Nine: Friday, October 4, 1918

All the Americans expected the impending battle to be hard. Intelligence analysts understood and valued how the German troops opposite the 1st Division had successfully counterattacked over this terrain and forced the 35th Division to withdraw. Now, under heavy pressure from the Big Red One, they were fighting harder than ever to defend the road to their homeland. German intelligence reported that Americans had behaved cautiously since September 29. They mistakenly believed the Americans would have to silence German artillery and flat trajectory fire along the Aire River before advancing.

Facing exhaustion, some German troops likely welcomed the possibility that the American advance might be delayed. Though the German 5th Division had succeeded in recapturing Côte de Montrebeau on the second day of the 35th Division offensive, September 27, it suffered from a great number of casualties and extended fighting. It had been rated a first-class division, but it lost half its men in June, then fought constantly throughout September. Observers later described it as growing exhausted and demoralized.[212]

Germans reported the weakened condition of the 5th Guards before the 1st Division came into the battle. In one instance, a battalion commander, just a 1st lieutenant, informed his commander that because of the extreme hardships suffered during the past month, his men had reached a serious stage of exhaustion. They could "scarcely be induced to stay in line," and in the event of an attack a brigade commander denied all responsibility for what "he knows will happen."[213]

All the 1st Division's battalion commanders assembled at 2300 on the night of October 3 to receive orders for the next day's attack across the ravines to Cote 240. Morale rose when the attack was ordered for October 4, though it would not be an easy battle. As part of the army-wide offensive, the 1st Division would pick up where the failed first phase of the Argonne offensive was left off; they would even attack past the bodies of the 35th Division's dead. High Command expected the 1st Division to play a key role, commanding that it would "put out a screen of men to the line of departure and advance to it at H hour," the hour for the planned attack.[214]

On the next morning they formed for attack. Brigades were abreast and regiments in columns of battalions. The huge Exermont Ravine, which consisted of a series of smaller ravines, was wide enough and deep enough to allow the three elements—attack, support and reserve—of each combat unit (company, battalion, regiment, and brigade) to line up one behind the other. This arrangement accommodated leapfrogging and passing through, which were by then established, tested infantry tactics. Everyone in the 1st Division knew those maneuvers from training and experience and believed they gave fresh impulse to assaults as battles progressed. Those tactics were especially useful as troops on the point wore down. Experience, cooperation, and practice made the system work.

The army-wide attack began on October 4 with the German 5th Guards Division directly opposite the 1st Brigade of the 1st Division. A wait of twenty-two minutes was scheduled between the planned attacks of the 1st and 2nd Brigades.[215]

The sky filled with German and American airplanes on the first morning.[216] Friendly US aircraft brought down one of the German planes, and anti-aircraft fire took another.[217] Seven American planes went over the line on the first day, and five were lost.[218] The Germans maintained air superiority then and throughout the entire Argonne campaign. This attack to cross the Exermont Ravine marked the beginning of what would be an eight-day, superhuman effort to drive a wedge through German defenses approaching and on top of the Romagne Heights.

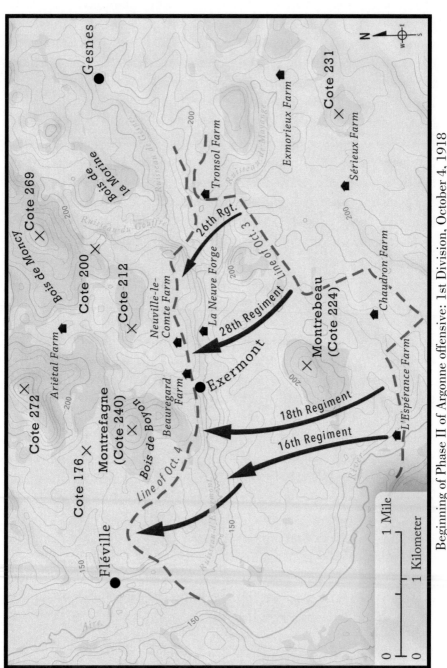

Beginning of Phase II of Argonne offensive: 1st Division, October 4, 1918

The 1st Brigade attacks on the first day, October 4

The 16th Infantry Regiment's 3rd Battalion and the 18th Infantry Regiment's 3rd Battalion led the 1st Brigade attack through the dark on the left of the 1st Division front. According to the plan, no preliminary artillery was fired.[219] Instead, "A smoke screen was placed along the southern edge of Cote 240 for thirty minutes before jump-off. The attack units advanced side by side at 0525. The support and reserve units followed. An extremely heavy German barrage came down from the jump-off line to about 1,000 meters behind it, causing quite a few casualties."[220] The 16th and 18th Infantry Regiments, about 6,500 men each, reached the Exermont Ravine, the first objective, at 0700. It was all small-group fighting after that, but the front remained continuous.[221]

The 6th Field Artillery Regiment supported the 1st Brigade with a thin barrage of about forty-eight guns for every five thousand yards.[222] Many of the unit's doughboys showed courage and resolve, both on October 4 and the following days. Despite having four wounds from a barrage that killed all but two artillerymen, 1st Lt. Samuel T. Smith returned to the site again and again to help evacuate the wounded.[223] Pvt. James W. Collier made his way forward to locate enemy artillery firing into his batteries at close range.[224] Cpl. Joseph F. Petrovic, of the 6th Artillery's Battery D, and another man survived a hit on their gun. After repairing the weapon, they continued firing. Two days later the gun was hit again, and Petrovic continued firing the mission after all other crew members received wounds.[225] Maj. Raymond B. Austin made numerous trips to gather target information and observe fire until he was killed on October 7.[226]

Heavy infantry fighting started when 1st Brigade troops came out of the ravine between Exermont and Gesnes, and hand-to-hand combat spread down the line.[227] German artillery concentrations laid down heavy fire that placed a wall of bursting fire ahead of the line.[228] A short gully from the ravine extended south almost exactly on the boundary between the 1st Brigade's two regiments. The Germans shielded themselves in the wooded area with excellent cover and concealment while firing into the attackers. Sgt. Elmer M. Marsh, Company K, took command of his portion of the attack after all officers were killed or wounded. He was severely wounded.[229]

The Americans took great personal risks, as Pvt. Donald Kyler of the 16th Infantry described:

> I crawled slowly from brush to brush to within easy grenade throwing range, took the grenades from my pockets, pulled the pins and threw them in rapid succession into the gulley where the enemy were. When the second grenade left my hand, I grabbed my rifle and rushed towards the edge. The grenades exploded just before I got there. One German turned toward me and I shot him without raising my rifle to my shoulder. Two more were at the machine gun, one perhaps wounded by a grenade. I jumped from the edge of the gully on the nearest German and thrust my bayonet deep into the other one. I could feel bones give way under my feet and I knew those three were finished. The other Germans fled and abandoned their equipment.[230]

Kyler's experience was not unique; men across the division faced similar challenges. Cptn. Harry J. Selby guided his 18th Infantry Battalion "through heavy artillery and machine-gun fire," drawing fire while others made a flank attack. He shot with his pistol until killed.[231] During the attack Cptn. John E. Martie lead his company forward, organized his position for defense, and held it against German counterattacks.[232] Pvt. George S. Johnson destroyed an enemy machine gun and took four prisoners.[233] Private First Class (PFC) Ben Kunieawsky and a companion advanced in search of machine guns. When his fellow soldier was killed, Kunieawsky advanced alone and found the machine gun, putting it out of action.[234] Sgt. Joseph Bradford, "consolidating remnants of other platoons with his....directed an attack against two nests, which were reduced."[235] Lt. Earl Almon, a battalion adjutant, lead the 16th Infantry's assault when the battalion commander and all officers became casualties. Despite his own wounds and incoming fire, Almon reorganized the battalion and continued the advance. The men gained and held the objective, withstanding two counterattacks in the process.[236]

Prisoners from the German 5th Guards reported being ordered to hold at all costs.[237] The size of a German division varied and, in this instance, it was an exhausted force of seventy-three officers and 1,568 enlisted men. Eight German divisions served in its famous Group Argonne, but only five of them, including the 5th, fought the Big Red One. In total the Germans numbered about 5,500.[238] Four of those divisions met the attack of the 1st Division as it crossed the Exermont Ravine, which was like a ditch nearly four miles long in front of a fortress.[239]

The creeping artillery barrage for the Americans fell into the ravine, followed by the 16th Infantry's 3rd Battalion and the 18th Infantry's 3rd Battalion.[240] These were not fresh troops, having been in the line and under fire for four days before the jump-off. On reaching open ground beyond the ravine they came under demoralizing machine gun fire from Cote 240. Meanwhile, from the ridges in the lead battalion's rear, a raking fire came from big guns beyond the Aire Valley.

Hill 240.

The 16th Infantry takes and holds Fléville

After reaching the ravine, the 16th Infantry's 2nd and 3rd Battalions headed to the left towards the village of Fléville, their next objective. Cptn. William R. McMorris directed his company's advance through intense machine gun and artillery fire. When the battalion commander was wounded, McMorris lead the battalion, acquiring his own wound during a German counterattack.[241] The 16th's attacking 2nd and 3rd Battalions suffered heavy losses on the approach to Fléville and were merged. Together they continued to make up less than a full battalion, but still they took Fléville at about 1300.

They then withdrew in anticipation of heavy German artillery, which promptly came in. The 16th Infantry covered more than five miles, ending up on high ground overlooking the ruins of the village and digging into the reverse slope of the hill on the south of Fléville. Although it gave good protection from the machine gun and rifle fire directly in front, it offered little protection from either flank, and it continued to catch the full force of Germans firing from the high ground west of the Aire River.[242] The river was narrow at that point, and across it stood the German-occupied Hill 180, directly in line with the 16th. The enemy fired point-blank into the American position. The shells came in a flat trajectory and gave no warning whine, just a quick shriek.

Though the challenging advance had necessitated combining battalions due to heavy losses, Kyler, who led a squad in the attack all day, viewed the situation differently, as often happens in combat situations. He said "The advance to Fléville had been relatively easy, but holding it was something else. The enemy had direct observation of our line. Much harassing long range machine gun fire was received from that direction until the 18th and 28th Infantries took the hills and their northern slopes."[243]

Many soldiers in the unit displayed heroics throughout the day. Working with five soldiers, Sgt. George V. Brown entered enemy territory, maintaining his position until help came, despite being surrounded by Germans and suffering from a gas attack.[244] Sgt. Luther Ruhl, Company F, 16th Infantry, assumed leadership when his platoon leader became a casualty. He "reorganized his platoon…and led it forward in a successful attack" against a machine gun nest.[245] Cpl. Max Seltzer, of Company M, single-handedly "silenced an enemy machine gun."[246] Cpl. Jesse W. Sargent, also of Company M, working alone in daylight and under fire, killed a machine gunner and assisted his unit's advance.[247] Sgt. Edward E. King assumed Company M's command "after its commander was wounded." After supplementing his unit with "remnants of other units," King led the men to Fléville. Consolidating the position, he led a patrol to clean out troublesome nests.[248] While serving as a messenger Pvt. William Gillespie received serious wounds but continued his mission and died after accomplishing it.[249]

Once in position south of Fléville, troops from the 16th Infantry were supported by a standing barrage fired directly in front of them for twenty minutes. Some single guns of the 6th and 7th Artillery regiments fired more than one thousand rounds in those first twenty-four hours.[250]

Second Lt. Edward L. Wells, 2nd Machine Gun Battalion, volunteered to enter the village of Exermont with a 16th Infantry platoon. With machine gun support, the men went through the village and captured prisoners, one of whom directed Wells to German machine gun sites. Before being killed, Wells shared the enemy's position with Americans in the rear.[251]

Summerall attached Company F of 1st Engineers to 1st Brigade, and under the cover of darkness they dug trenches and built protection for the infantry.[252] Facing enemy on three sides, the nearest friendly troops on the left were at least two kilometers in the rear.[253] The men spent the night in their holes and achieved the honor of being the only 1st Army unit to reach its final objective on the first day of fighting.[254]

They had succeeded in driving a wedge into the German position, but success came at great price. The two battalions counted 2 officers and 240 men remaining of the 20 officers and 800 men who had joined the assault that morning.[255] Parts of the merged 2nd and 3rd Battalions remained at the base of Cote 240, while some companies were positioned on the hill. Those on the open plain south of Fléville caught the full force of German artillery and flat trajectory fire from Cote 180, which was southwest of them along the Aire. The entire 16th Infantry force simply fought to hold on.

With his unit running short of food, Kyler, later wrote, "I was ordered to take a small carrying party to a supply point in the rear." Having found canned goods, he told the men, "Hold on to those cans as you would your life. If you hold on to those cans the Germans may shoot you, but drop one and I sure will. And don't think that I won't." Reflecting further on his wartime experiences, Kyler recalled, "I was 17 ½ years old. At no time had I ever been away from the sound of battle."[256]

Though the 16th Infantry had been victorious in meeting its day's objective, such success had a price. Because other parts of the division had been less successful, the 16th held its position while hoping that flanking 1st Division units would draw even.

The 18th Regiment fights on the west end of Hill 240

Between September 30 and October 4, the 18th Regiment had 459 dead and 1,277 wounded—a staggering number of casualties that represented nearly half the size of a typical regiment.[257] Therefore, the regiment was shorthanded when it jumped off into the Exermont Ravine at 0525 in two waves of two companies behind rolling artillery fire. There was no preliminary bombardment. Flat land north of the ravine contained the village of Exermont, and just above the village was the enemy's first line of defense, which stood on the southern edge of Cote 240. Machine gun and artillery positions there swept the area from the ravine across to Exermont. The whole regiment would have to advance through this area before it could reach Hill 240, and its men fought every foot of the way. They met resistance and crossed machine gun trenches, wiping them out in fifteen minutes. They also bayonetted some of the gunners, showing the excellent quality of German troops.[258] Soldiers entering the village of Exermont initially received fire from the rear, but they soon drove the Germans out, allowing other 18th Infantry soldiers to reach the southern slope of Cote 240.

The 18th's regimental line extended around Cote 240 to the west and the south, practically flanking the hill. Bois de Boyon stood between the ravine and the hill. The attacking infantrymen passed the bodies of 1st Division men killed on patrols. Fully exposed, the unit could not bury its dead, and litter bearers could not get all the wounded off the battlefield. The battalion aid station made three forward moves during the day, and every enlisted medic was killed or wounded.

Many of the 18th's men demonstrated heroics during the day. After all officers became casualties, Cpl. Leonard Cavanaugh assumed command of his company, leading its attack on Hill 240.[259] Cptn. Dallas R. Alfonte was wounded and stayed in a position under enemy observation on Hill 240 "until his regiment was relieved."[260] After the 2nd Battalion commander went missing, Lt. Arthur B. Cornwell led the unit forward, allowing flanking units on the right and left to continue their advance as scheduled.[261] The unit joined the fighting after crossing the ravine and halted for reorganization after reaching the base of Hill 240. Because a gap was developing between the 16th and 18th Infantry Regiments, Cornwell's regiment then extended to the left and connected with the right of the two merged 16th Infantry battalions at Fléville.[262]

After advancing through the trees on the base of Hill 240's south slope, elements of the 18th Infantry reached the top of the hill. The fresh 1st Battalion came up to guard against counterattacks. The 2nd Battalion dug in just above it, and the 3rd Battalion camped on the south slope at the base of Hill 240. They remained there until withdrawing, returning to the bottom to spend the night better protected.[263]

The 2nd Brigade crosses the Exermont Ravine on the southeast, the right of Cote 240

Brig. Gen. Frank Bamford's 2nd Brigade formed the right flank of the division-wide attack. Final orders arrived at 0300 the morning of October 4. Summerall instructed the 2nd Brigade to get on the crest of Cote 240, take the woods north of Cote 212, and come in line with the 1st Brigade.[264] Before dawn, men in the 26th and 28th Regiments rolled their packs, preparing for jump-off to cross the Exermont Ravine. The attacking regiments were led by rolling fire from the 7th Field Artillery, after which its guns were pointed towards the east end of Cote 240.[265]

The 26th and 28th Infantry Regiments formed side by side with the 1st Brigade's 18th Infantry on their left. The 2nd Brigade's point battalions were the 28th Infantry's 3rd Battalion on the left and the 26th Infantry's 1st Battalion on the right. They comingled and pushed across the eastern end of the ravine behind a rolling barrage. From the beginning they had a fight on their hands, with especially heavy fire from the Neuville–le-Comte Farm until they took that position.[266]

Soldiers going forward in the regiments delivered very little rifle fire in the fog and concentrated on staying close to the rolling artillery barrage all the way to Cote 240.[267] The Germans put up a stubborn defense but lost much of their first line in fifteen minutes. Americans shot and bayonetted many of their gunners.[268]

The Germans had several batteries of 77 mm guns about a thousand yards north of the ravine. The 28th Infantry's 3rd Battalion captured the guns and turned them on the enemy.[269] However, the attacking Americans were stopped short of the division's second objective line, which started near the southern part of Fléville.[270] The enemy showed stubborn resistance and handled its artillery well but suffered heavy losses.[271]

The 28th Infantry's Company M then prepared to defend the exposed right flank if the Germans attacked there, which happened. Company M faced a rear guard of German machine gunners, but the Germans went nowhere, as Company M succeeded in sealing the right flank.

Machine gun companies of about two hundred men went forward under orders from the infantry battalion commanders to which they were assigned. Each regiment and each brigade had a fully formed machine gun company that reported directly to the regimental commander, a full colonel, or to the brigade commander, a brigadier general.

Each infantry battalion and machine gun battalion held its own doctrine for machine gun fighting. Some believed in and experimented with indirect fire. Others wanted machine guns to be used as flat trajectory weapons carried forward by hand. Still others wanted them to dig in at the jump-off line to be saved for a German counterattack, making the guns useful only as defensive weapons in such situations.

The 3rd Machine Gun Battalion's Company A was attached to the 26th Infantry's 3rd Battalion on the point. Many believed that the 1st Division had never handled machine gun companies more aggressively and skillfully than in this attack. 2nd Brigade's 3rd Machine Gun Battalion was deployed as a tactical unit reaching the Exermont Ravine. Then it offered more strategic barrage fire, with twenty-four guns delivering indirect overhead fire in support of the advancing 26th and 28th Regiments.[272]

Division artillery assigned two French 75s and a crew-served 37mm gun to each attacking infantry battalion. The 26th Infantry used ropes to pull forward its own 37 mm guns on wheels. Other crew members carried as much ammunition as they could.[273] The 37mm always served as an offensive weapon, typically positioned close to the enemy. It was usually so close that incoming German 77mm rounds exploded before the 37mm crew heard the shots.

Six three-inch Stokes mortars, called stove pipes, were organic (an army term meaning a permanently assigned) to each regiment and were assigned to infantry battalions by regimental headquarters. These guns, which delivered high angle of fire at close range, required a loader and an observer or spotter to adjust fire. The battalions usually relied on mortars more in offensive operations than in defensive ones, but tactics varied by unit and according to the terrain and situation.

Going rapidly through early morning fog in the dark, the 2nd Brigade's 6,500 men followed the rolling barrage. They were stopped by heavy machine gun fire at the Exermont Ravine and another ravine south of it, the Ruisseau de Mayange. The 26th Infantry Regiment entered the ravine with thirty officers and about a thousand men before reaching the northern edge with six officers and 285 men. Despite the massive casualties, the regiment kept the attack alive.[274]

Maj. Rice Youell, who had been wounded—but not evacuated—on the first day, led his men in taking the hills beyond Ruisseau du Gouffre.[275] Maj. Frasier, the commander of the 3rd Battalion, which had started as the reserve battalion, was wounded but not evacuated.[276]

Control of artillery was passed from its artillery fire direction center to the infantry regimental and brigade commanders. This way of operating proved most effective, as it facilitated cooperation and understanding, but it was possible only because of superior liaison arrangements between infantry and artillery commanders and the fire direction centers. An artillery liaison officer served with the assault battalion commanders as well as with the regimental commanders.[277]

The artillery was responsible for laying its own telephone lines and maintaining them with their own linemen. A signal pack train was nearly wiped out when Sgt. Lawernce Lumpkin drove his animals forward with loads of telephone wire. He lost five of his ten mules before continuing the mission.[278]

In the beginning of the attack, communication was all by written field messages, which were carried by runners until telephone lines could be laid atop the ground. Organization charts called for four runners in each rifle company, but companies rarely operated at full strength, and runners were always in short supply. Telephone linemen followed close behind infantry battalion commanders, who were delivering field messages. Standard procedure was to use written field messages for only the first six hours of battle, but army doctrine required companies to keep battalions informed at all times, just as battalions had to update regiments. The runner system worked but was costly, and two runners traveling separate routes carried all important messages. Seventy-four 1st Division runners were killed or wounded during the Argonne fighting.[279]

Though the casualties mounted, many 2nd Brigade soldiers displayed great valor. Lt. Stuart A. Baxter, wounded, crawled forward under fire to aid his unit.[280] Second Lt. George J. Forster directed the 26th Infantry's 37mm guns, while Sgt. Lain Dobbs and a few other men of its Company B were surrounded by approximately fifty Germans.[281] Dobbs and his men killed and wounded many before forcing the others to withdraw. Though gassed, Dobbs fought until acquiring serious shellfire wounds.[282] Using a pistol, Cpl. Thomas J. O'Keefe killed a number of Germans before he was killed.[283]

Cptn. Howard F. Hawkinson led the regiment's assault battalion in the jump-off. In darkness with his staff, he took fire from a German detachment with two machine guns. Advancing with his pistol, he fell mortally wounded ten yards from a machine gun nest.[284] Cpl. Byron C. Echols led the 3rd Machine Gun Battalion ahead of the infantry line and silenced two machine guns before being severely wounded.[285] Sgt. Frederick R. Cushing of Battery C, 7th Field Artillery, took his artillery piece forward to the infantry line, where despite taking violent fire, he refused to withdraw until "nearly all his horses and three of his men were wounded." After withdrawing, he made five trips to evacuate the wounded.[286]

The 28th Infantry Regiment comes out of the ravine and fights on the right

Germans nearly annihilated the 28th Infantry's 3rd Battalion after it crossed the ravine and arrived in the vicinity of the Neuville-le-Comte Farm. The group came under direct fire from 77mm guns at a range of about eight hundred yards. In a line, the regiment crossed the valley southeast of Cote 240 and advanced to a position running from the Beauregard Farm to the Neuville-le-Comte Farm.[287] The objective was an imaginary line from the base of what the 1st Division history referred to as the "great forbidding ridge of Cote 272 to Cote 212."[288] The heavily fortified Cote 272 gave Germans unobscured observation for their artillery. The 28th captured the German battery on the line of German troops that ran from the Beauregard Farm to the Neuville-le-Comte Farm, then occupied the line.[289]

Men of the 28th demonstrated valor and courage throughout the day. Cpl. Fritzhof Langemak, Company M, "assumed command of [his] platoon in the absence of any commissioned officer." Though most of the men were replacements, Langemak reorganized them and led them against enemy machine gun nests without knowledge of the platoon's location or maps to guide them.[290] Pvt. Sterling Morelock, a messenger in Company M, 28th Infantry, organized three other runners at company headquarters into a patrol when his company was held up. He led them through fire to penetrate woods forming the German front line at the base of Cote 240. Taking out five machine gun nests and fighting until he was seriously hurt and all his men were casualties, Morelock evacuated the group along with ten captured Germans who served as stretcher bearers. He received the Congressional Medal of Honor for his actions.[291]

The Germans had good shooting from Cote 212 into the right side of 2nd Brigade as it attacked towards Cote 272. German heavy artillery reached beyond the first line of assault battalions into the American support and reserve battalions further back. The line of attack stretched to woods north of Cote 212 and to the base of the big hill, Cote 272—both formidable objectives.[292] The entire zone of attack came under German artillery fire. The 28th Infantry, ordered to top the crest of Cote 240 on the first day, failed to do so.

Russian-born Pvt. Stanley Gancaz, Company I, 28th Infantry, joined by Pvt. George W. Garner and Cpl. Berte L. Kinkade, silenced a German 77mm gun and captured its crew. They swept nearby German dugouts, capturing another forty prisoners.[293]

The 2nd Brigade's 26th Infantry Regiment fights on Hill 240

The 26th Infantry, commanded by Col. Hjalmar Erickson, took its position on the far right in the division attack. Its exposed right flank took some fire but no serious attack from that direction. The regiment jumped off at 0525 on October 4, navigating by compass, and failed to keep up with the rolling barrage, which put a German 77mm out of action, across the Exermont Ravine. Because their crossing point was narrow—about 200 yards wide and 120 feet deep—the incoming fire forced the men to advance forward in narrow squad columns rather than waves.

The 1st Battalion led the assault with the 2nd in support and the 3rd in reserve. Scouts kept the advancing infantry files aligned with flanking units. The regiment advanced in a file strung out for nearly a mile with all three battalions in a column of battalions. They divided into columns of companies and platoons, one behind the other.[294] The gas unit put up smoke on the southern edge of Cote 240 for thirty minutes after the jump-off, and the 1st Battalion on the point benefited from concealment by smoke and fog so heavy in places men could not see fifty yards ahead.[295] However, the Germans could see everything when the smoke lifted. Then the 1st Division artillery and infantry had no choice but to fight in the open under heavy German fire from the crest of Cote 212 and the woods beyond.[296] The 26th Infantry met fierce resistance in the ravine and after crossing it. The enemy fought very hard, and few surrendered.[297]

At jump-off, the 2nd Battalion made an impressive sight. As 2nd Lt. William A. Mansfield, 26th Infantry, recorded, "As far as vision permitted . . . a wave of khaki clothed men with bayonets at the 'high carry' were moving forward as on maneuvers."[298] The rear of battalion columns crossing the ravine shifted from a column of companies and platoons into squad columns in order to provide more scattered targets, but German fire badly depleted the 1st Battalion by the time it finally got across the ravine.[299] The 2nd Battalion fared similarly, entering the Exermont Ravine with thirty officers and a thousand men but reaching the northern side with only six officers and 285 men.[300]

Once in the clear, the 26th Infantry faced Cote 212. Woods covered the reverse slope of Cote 212 as troops moved in the direction of Cote 200 on the far right of the division boundary. The 26th focused on capturing a small strip of woods on a line about seven hundred meters east of the Neuville-le-Comte Farm, taking all day to get it done. German machine gun emplacements stood along the wood's edge, and the 26th's assault and support battalions faced fire from the front, from the right flank, and from the Neuville-le-Comte and Beauregard Farms. That fire persisted until the 28th Infantry took the position on their left in a relief effort that involved hand-to-hand fighting.

American artillery observers on the front "sensed" (an artillery term meaning they estimated the accuracy) their rounds while making corrections by telephone and referring to grid coordinates on maps. Some batteries fired at rates of up to ten shots a minute. The 26th's 1st Battalion had good artillery support but did not advance the line quickly after the initial push.[301] Everybody was relieved when they saw the artillery move forward, a sign that the American battle was doing well.[302]

The 1st Battalion commander recalled, "After unsuccessful efforts to maneuver left and right of Ruisseau de Mayange I had lost practically all of the officers and suffered about 50% casualties."[303] The support battalion, the 2nd, passed through the assault battalion to lead the assault at about 1315.[304] It then occupied a space about four hundred yards deep and eight hundred yards wide. The 2nd Brigade's 3rd Machine Gun Battalion joined in by firing an indirect fire mission on the Tronsol Farm and successfully suppressed small arms coming from there.[305]

Heavy German fire from Cote 240 hit the 26th Infantry's position to the south side, and the regiment also took fire from the Ariétal Farm.[306] The regimental commander sent a 37mm gun to the 1st Battalion's commander. A machine gun company reported to the 3rd Battalion commander offering support. By working forward the crew of the 37mm gun section put it into action against Germans in the Tronsol Farm. At the end of the day the 26th Infantry's 1st and 2nd Battalions set up a defense on their right. The area was strongly held by the enemy, as was a wooded area called the Bois de la Morine.

The 26th Infantry suffered heavy casualties in hard fighting on October 4.[307] Sgt. Alexander Gosselin, 2nd Signal Battalion, was killed after ordering his men to shelter while he remained to repair wire breaks caused by artillery.[308] Cptn. Raymond Wortley was killed while commanding the 2nd Battalion. Cptn. Hamilton K. Foster and Lt. Harry Dillon were both killed leading their companies across the Exermont Valley.[309]

Division supply elements functioned well.[310] The 2nd and 3rd Hospitals pushed hard and treated more than 1,600 people on October 4. Despite suffering heavy casualties and failing to reach its final objective line, the 1st Division had much to be proud of at the end of the day. No other 1st Army division had advanced further or penetrated deep into the German lines.

Though the 1st Division found some success, other divisions struggled. Pershing sent the 29th and 33rd Divisions to capture the Meuse Heights, but they struggled to drive the German machine-gunners from the high ground, and it remained in enemy hands for another week. In the Argonne, the 77th Division was also slowed by German defenses that were hard to penetrate in the deep woods. A composite battalion from the 77th Division's 307th and 308th Infantry Regiments advanced beyond the units on its flanks and found itself cut off and trapped in the forest for five days. Though the stand of this "Lost Battalion" would become one of the storied moments of the Meuse-Argonne campaign, its outcome was by no means certain on the evening of October 4.

Such challenges made the 1st Division's progress that day all the more important. Pershing wanted to keep up the momentum and ordered the division to attack again the next day.

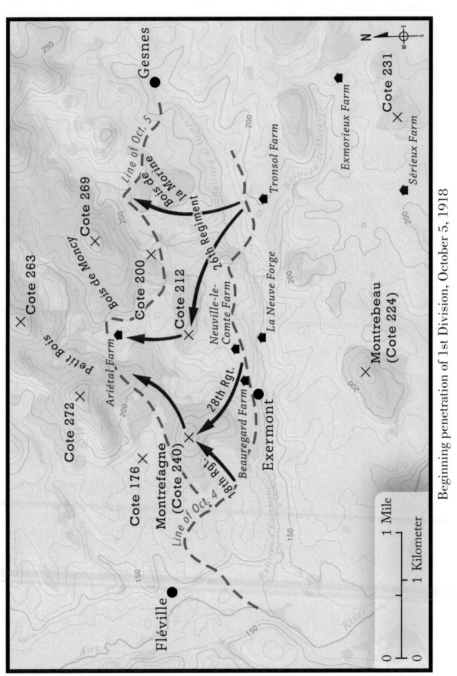

Beginning penetration of 1st Division, October 5, 1918

CHAPTER 3

Stalemate Beyond the Exermont Ravine

Day Ten: Saturday, October 5, 1918

After crossing the Exermont Ravine on October 4, the 1st Division's 16th and 18th Infantry Regiments lined up on the left, with the 28th and 26th Infantry Regiments on the right with both facing Cote 240.[311] The division ordered its two brigades to take the crest of Cote 240 and even up the division front line.

The 28th's 3rd Battalion and the 18th's 3rd Battalion were ordered to attack uphill and take Cote 240 by different routes. Elements of the 18th had made it to the crest of Cote 240 on the previous day, but they retreated to the hill's south base that night. General Summerall ordered them to return to the crest the next day, so the southern edge of the forest at the base of Cote 240 became the front line for their second day of fighting.

The 16th Infantry holds on at Fléville

Because the 16th Infantry had already taken Fléville, it spent the day working to hold the village, turning back a serious counterattack by several hundred Germans. Many German dead and wounded were left on the perimeter of the 16th's position. Though the regiment's overall status remained relatively static throughout the day, holding the position was no small feat and contained substantial action.

Private Kyler, still on the defense line at Fléville with four others and a corporal, later recorded his account of the day's drama. After describing feeling "benumbed" by the counterattack, Kyler explained how the Germans advanced and eventually fell back after repeated and aggressive fire from the Americans. His description of the skirmish's aftermath offers a poignant view of the tolls of war:

> All over that open ground to the front of us there were
> wounded and dying men. . . . Five of us remained firing
> to the last. . . . I was nearly exhausted. . . . my right
> shoulder was bruised from having absorbed the recoil of
> my rifle so many times, my left hand was burned, my
> right eye, cheek and chin were bruised by being bumped
> by my rifle during firing. . . . That night. . . we kept
> hearing wounded Germans to the front of our position
> crying out in their misery. A young soldier from Montana
> . . . sprang up and said that he would make them shut up.
> He took his bayonet and silently crept forward between
> our outposts. In a little while the cries ceased and he came
> back. Our attitude was that they were better off than we
> were. Their misery was over.[312]

With great effort, the 16th had held Fléville.

The 18th and 28th Regiments take Montrefagne (Hill 240)

General Summerall's plan for the attacking 1st and 2nd Brigades
had been to take everything from the jump-off position to a point
halfway to Cote 272. Therefore, as the 16th labored to keep Fléville
in Allied hands, the 18th and 28th Infantry Regiments, despite heavy
losses, began making the "slow and painful advance up the bare,
open ridge leading to Hill 240."[313]

Artillery was to be fired two hundred meters in front of the line
of departure at H hour minus five minutes. Though artillery had
authority to use gas, its only gas plan involved smoke. Artillery fire
was ordered to soften up the Germans on the first objective, a line
passing along the south edge of Cote 240.[314]

The 18th and 28th approached Hill 240 at the same time, but they
used different routes. The 28th's attack up the south side of Cote 240
started with small-unit fighting. During its advance, the 28th's 3rd
Battalion stopped briefly on the crest of Hill 240 while under German
observation from Cote 272.[315] It continued over the crest until
reaching the low ground on the north base of Cote 240.[316]

Fog blanketed the area, and communication was difficult. A German document captured at noon reported, "under cover of fog, enemy renewed heavy attacks between Aire and Exermont, fighting in Fléville, Montrefagne...still under way."[317]

The 28th attacked from Cote 240 in the direction of Cote 272, with the 3rd Battalion leapfrogging the 1st until stopped by German 77 and machine gun fire from Cotes 176 and 272. After being slowed by fire from Cote 272, the 3rd Battalion tried to go forward again that afternoon. It took heavy losses in this first of five 1st Division attacks on Cote 272. The 18th's 2nd Battalion also got into the battle after reaching the northern slope of Cote 240 and heading towards Cote 272. Like the 28th's 3rd Battalion, it was stopped by fire from Cotes 272 and 176.

Troops laid no wire until after crossing the Exermont Ravine, so all communications until then traveled via messengers. Signal Corps men took great risks to lay wire on top of the ground. Sgt. Dennis H. Lockard led a wire repair "detail through intense bombardment" and maintained essential communication between the firing line and the regiment's commander.[318] Cptn. George Cox of 2nd Field Signal Battalion conducted "hazardous daylight reconnaissance" and, with assistance from two others, ensured that Hill 240 had telephone communication.[319] Cpl. Waldo Thompson advanced under fire to repair telephone lines that the infantry and artillery used to communicate.[320] After laying wire, the Signal Corps men were to maintain the connections, but despite their efforts, no telephone communication existed between the forward battalions.[321]

In both brigades the 1st sergeants formed a straggler line behind the attacking regiments to be sure casuals stayed fully engaged. This minimized cowardice and running from the enemy.[322]

Despite `the concern for casuals, many 28th Infantry soldiers earned honors for their valiant conduct. During the action Sgt. Michael B. Ellis, 28th Infantry, Company C, advanced alone. He killed two and captured twenty-seven Germans and six machine guns, earning him the Congressional Medal of Honor.[323] First Lt. Coleman E. O'Flaherty, a Catholic chaplain, had been routinely exposing himself to fire while treating wounded during the attacks. "Under terrific fire," he was killed during this latest assault.[324] Pvt. James Lewis consistently volunteered for patrols and was "placed in permanent command of his platoon."[325] Cpl. Elmer L. Norris knocked out a machine gun and captured the crew.[326] Second Lt. William H. Barry earned a Distinguished Service Cross for his October 5 actions, which included taking over his company's command after it suffered many losses, leading the reorganized men, and gaining their objective.[327] Cpl. David B. Stewart Jr., Company D, advanced a hundred yards ahead of his company in search of machine gun positions and captured twelve Germans.[328] After his company was stopped, Cptn. James V. Ware reorganized the remaining sixty-three men, leading their second attack to take the enemy position at the point of a bayonet.[329] Sgt. Thomas D. Curfman "took an automatic rifle from a wounded gunner and went forward alone," destroying a German machine gun nest before being mortally wounded.[330] With only his pistol, 2nd Lt. Samuel I. Parker "advanced directly on a machine gun 150 yards away...and killed the gunner."[331]

Soldiers in other units also demonstrated heroics during the attacks. Maj. Ewing M. Taylor, 18th Infantry, Company B, "advanced his machine guns" until he was wounded amid heavy fire.[332] After capturing machine gun nests on both October 4 and 5, the 18th's Sgt. Stanley F. Cerbin assumed Company H's command when all its officers became casualties.[333] During a mission to rescue six men, Lt. Charles F. Warren, also of the 18th, led his platoon forward through fire, urging soldiers to follow him, until he was wounded by machine gun fire.[334] Pvt. George Strawbridge, 2nd Machine Gun Battalion, administered first aid to the wounded and refused evacuation upon incurring his own wounds; he stayed with his company throughout the operation.[335] Another soldier in the 2nd Machine Gun Battalion, 2nd Lt. Theodore Bushnell, also insisted on staying with his platoon, despite his being wounded. He helped his men until being wounded once more.[336]

These men displayed heroism in intense conditions that garnered official notice. Cptn. William D. Haselton from Division headquarters visited front line units that day and wrote, "The character of the fighting was as bitter as any engaged in by the troops of the Allies in the entire AEF." He spent the day inspecting units over a ten-mile area while under high explosive fire and gas. He had mud splattered on him half a dozen times and splinters screaming by. He explained, "I ran from shell hole to shell hole to get to the other side of the ravine, shells fell faster than ever. I was in that kind of fire for an hour and a half and they dropped half a dozen gas shells in a valley I had to cross." He walked ten or eleven miles continuing his units' inspection. When he got back to headquarters, he realized how much he appreciated being able to have such a soft job in a quiet and safe place.[337]

Though they lacked the comforts available at headquarters, the men did enjoy a few amenities that evening. As scheduled, machine gun carts brought the large marmite cans used to serve the men their supper.[338] Mail also reached troops that night, boosting morale.

The 26th Infantry attacks Cotes 212 and 272 on October 5

While other soldiers of the 1st Division fought to the west of the line on October 5, the 26th Infantry Regiment had its own objective. Major Frasier, Commander of the 26th's 3rd Battalion, reported from Division Reserve to the regimental commander at 0300. They were in the small valley opening into the Ruisseau de Mayange southwest of the Tronsol Farm when he received verbal instructions to attack Cote 272 along with the regiment's other two battalions. Wire cutters from the engineers were sent forward in preparation for the move to Cote 212, to which they were to cut four paths.[339]

At 0600 a lieutenant from the 7th Field Artillery reported to Frasier with a horse-drawn 75mm gun. Going into position on Cote 240 to support the men advancing on Cote 272, he received fire from three directions: a forest named the Bois de Moncy, the hills west of the Aire, and Cote 272.[340] In a short time the Germans destroyed the 75mm and killed the officer, just as had happened to the 75mm and its commander supporting the 26th's 1st Battalion the previous morning. Therefore, no artillery fire supported the 3rd Battalion as it leapfrogged the 1st Battalion and moved towards Cote 272. The battalion was also supposed to be supported by six tanks, which had passed through the battalion that morning on their way to assist in the assault. Not one survived to reach the assault battalion before jump-off time. Before the attack even began, its plan had been compromised.

The weather did offer a bit of initial assistance, however. Smoke and heavy fog offered concealment from the beginning of the attack until about 0700. After that the 3rd Battalion came under full German observation and heavy German artillery and machine gun fire from the Bois de Moncy. The battalion started advancing from the east part of Cote 240 and met strong resistance.[341]

Approximately every twenty minutes, a deadly barrage from four German machine guns in front of Cote 212 opened up, lasting about three minutes. The American attack formation changed from broad waves to squads in columns. Moving fast, the front grew to seven hundred yards across and six hundred feet deep. Control was good despite their being no heavily wooded areas to offer cover and concealment. When the fog lifted Germans could see Americans descend into the valley east of the St. Germain Farm in squad columns.[342]

At 0900 the American advance stopped when hit by German artillery from Cote 272. Going by squads in single files instead of waves meant that the troops were less visible but required scouts to direct the files. Sometimes the battalion bunched up, the advance stopped, and the battalion scout officer went ahead alone. Some scouts were killed while trying to connect the files.

Throughout the morning, German movement continued on the edge of Côte de Moncy, also known as Cote 265. Communication was only by messenger.[343] The two attacking American battalions, the 26th's 1st and 3rd, were practically on the same ground. Progress slowed, and casualties were heavy.[344] By 1100 the 2nd Battalion reached its objective on Cote 212.

Cote 212 fell completely by noon, though 1st Battalion suffered heavy losses from enemy-held woods to the north.[345] Though it started with nearly one thousand men, it now held only two officers and 118 men. One officer and approximately twenty of the men had wounds.[346]

The platoon leader of the 37mm guns described it as a slow battle, "vicious in the extreme."[347] A machine gun platoon and two platoons of infantry then moved from Cote 212 to Cote 200.

An American barrage was scheduled on German positions for 1345, and the forty-five-minute wait for it tested 3rd Battalion nerves. The regimental commander messaged, "I am now calling for the rolling barrage to start. Follow this barrage when it starts and notify me when you reach the objective." Major Legge replied, "We will go thru if such a thing is possible." He added, "If the 32nd were fully up on our right it would go much better." Legge trusted the more familiar 1st Division soldiers more than he did the 32nd Division troops covering his right flank.[348] Because unit loyalty was strong, people from another unit were never trusted as much as people from one's own, even though the officers might not know all the men within their unit.[349]

Germans across the valley let off heavy machine gun and rifle fire.[350] Machine guns from the 1st and 3rd Battalions raked the German position in return, while the battalions' 37mm guns dueled with the Germans at four hundred yards. A German 77 fired eleven rounds into the Americans, knocking out a machine gun and a 37mm. The American 37mm section, working from camouflaged foxholes, took casualties, though American observers saw German machine gunners falling on empty shells, and a German field piece was destroyed by the remaining 37s.[351] Incoming German fire continued from the Bois de Moncy on the hills west of the Aire, Cote 272, and Cote 240.[352]

As the Germans killed and wounded American leaders, the platoon sergeants, squad leaders, and soldiers of the line took their places.[353] Cpl. Charles A. McCoy assumed command of Company I after its officers were wounded, though he was wounded himself. He reorganized the men and fought on in the face of machine gun fire.[354] After his leader's death, Pvt. Frank Dugan assumed section command, leading the men and "capturing three machine guns and crews."[355]

According to the Division Attack Order dated October 2, which stated that the line was to move forward with all the 6th and 7th Field Artillery Batteries, the 7th Regiment moved most of its guns forward to positions in the Ruisseau de Mayange, providing welcome evidence of the general attack's success.[356] An infantryman said, "The sight of that moving line of artillery was one of the memories of the war I shall not forget."[357]

The 26th's 3rd Battalion passed through its 1st Battalion to reach the assault line for the attack. Suddenly there was no time to lose. There was no reorganizing, no waiting for the scheduled barrage, no choice but to rush across the valley and close with the enemy, the only hope for the battalion to have concealment and cover. The 3rd Battalion's front line rushed down the slopes of Cote 212 into the bare valley. Companies L and M crossed in squad columns, double timing across the three hundred yards and taking cover in the finger of the valley of the Petit Bois. "There was no use for scouts now," Frasier recalled, "We knew exactly where the enemy was. He knew exactly where we were."[358] Company I advanced to a position four hundred yards from Cote 272, and Company K crossed the valley and fought up the right slope. By 1400 the 3rd Battalion occupied the Ariétal Farm. That confused the enemy on the right rear of the battalion, but at 1500 it appeared to be recovering and preparing for a counterattack. The battalion managed to advance on the left. The 3rd Battalion's Company I advanced to within two hundred yards of the hill, but none went further than the commander. He fell sixty yards from the woods of 272 with a bullet in his head. Companies L and M then crossed the valley in front of the hill by running three hundred yards in the open while under fire. As Frasier later described, "The second wave was decimated and soon became assimilated with the first wave."[359]

After crossing the valley, Companies I and K deployed with three lines of skirmishers at intervals of about ten yards. The first two lines merged into one, while two pieces of German artillery on the edge of the Petit Bois fired point-blank into the attackers. Frasier recollected that "sheets of steel from machine guns on the other side of the valley swept knee high over the ground, mowing down the advancing ranks and killing them after they fell."[360]

One of Frasier's companies broke and ran towards the rear, but two squads were held in place by their company commander.

Another company had begun retreating when a runner reached it with a message from the battalion commander ordering it to hold in place—an order they obeyed. The panicked men of Company M retreated, running past their battalion commander, but they were quickly stopped by three non-commissioned officers.

Telephone communication for battalions to regimental headquarters were put in place throughout the day, requiring an individual signal man to face exposure while splicing breaks for every five hundred yards of wire. However, some communications still traveled by messenger rather than phone. Two runners were sent by separate routes to the regimental command post with orders for the artillery liaison officer to bring fire on German machine guns in the valley, where the Germans advanced in a counterattack.[361]

While the 3rd Battalion crossed the valley in front of Cote 212 and advanced through the finger of the valley of the Petit Bois, the 3rd Machine Gun Battalion's Company A delivered heavy overhead fire to the edge of the Petit Bois and into the valley north of the Ariétal Farm. Artillery lifted fire as the troops advanced, bayoneting German artillerymen, and finally reaching Cote 272 while under enemy mortar and machine gun fire. After crossing the valley, the battalion engaged in hand-to-hand fighting at the Ariétal Farm and in the Bois de Moncy. A few groups of Germans tried to escape into the woods, but not more than a dozen reached them and few survived.[362]

Artillery requested for Company M came down on Cotes 272 and 263, but some of it fell on the 3rd Battalion's Company K, which was trying to get to Cote 263. It killed or wounded around forty men. While receiving that friendly fire, about 120 men retreated back across the hard-won valley. Though they had no orders to do so, no one criticized their choice. Thirty-five deadly minutes elapsed during this 3rd Battalion attack on Cote 272. Nine battalion officers and 150 men were killed.[363]

The Americans who had not retreated took cover in the Petit Bois, where they were supported by fire called in by the battalion commander's artillery liaison officer. He telephoned fire commands to the firing battery located in the Ruisseau de Mayange, southwest of the Neuville-le-Comte Farm. That shooting required guns in the Ruisseau de Mayange to fire missions aimed in three directions. Such complex artillery work was possible due to the division's innovative arrangement for artillery control, which bypassed the typical middlemen involved in such requests.[364] The fire destroyed several German machine guns and two artillery pieces, as well as targets in front of the 3rd Battalion and in the Bois de Moncy.

The 3rd Battalion launched another attack on Cote 272 at 1600, but it failed. The Germans cut down three waves of men as they came out of the woods.[365] Frasier faced an increasingly precarious situation. As darkness approached, his 3rd Battalion was down to three officers, two of whom were wounded, and about 180 effectives. Company M had scattered, and one its missing platoons would not be recovered until four days later.[366] Still, part of the company steadied and reorganized, doing its best to prepare for what was to come. Company K had no officers, no non-commissioned officers, and only twenty-eight privates left that night.[367] Company L positioned six machine guns around itself and continued gathering and organizing more soldiers to meet the expected German counterattack. Fortunately for the Americans, that counterattack never came. However, the battalion suffered losses from patrols; one went out at 2200 to reconnoiter the front of Cote 272, and another departed at 2330 to reconnoiter the Germans' left flank.

Regimental headquarters ordered the advance stopped, and a 75mm moved up. The battalion asked for food, water, and ten thousand rounds of machine gun ammunition. No food or water came up that night. The men had reserve rations, but regulations forbade them from eating those unless they had been taken from the dead. Until it rained, canteens held the only available water. Men could not drink water from shell holes due to poison-gas residual, but their shelter halves caught some water.

Casualties caused the seven-hundred-yard front to thin out. The right assault company, Company K, stood on the right flank of Cote 272. The huge hill ran east–west across the sector, and its crest reached 221 feet above the plain. The Germans occupying it had unobstructed vision and a clear field of fire up to, behind, and to either side of Cote 240. Covered with well-hidden German machine guns, Cote 272 held many unexposed enemy mortars with high angles of fire to meet the advancing 3rd Battalion. Despite its hard fighting, heavy casualties, and a gain of about fifteen hundred yards, the 3rd Battalion did not reach its objective, Cote 272.[368]

In fighting that day each soldier fired about two hundred rounds per rifle and about 4,800 rounds from each machine gun, both unusually high numbers. While soldiers were usually reluctant to shoot, officers encouraged the heavy fire by telling men they could only save their own lives by killing the enemy.[369]

Throughout the 1st Division attacks, soldiers in the 2nd Machine Gun Battalion acted valiantly in the face of severe casualties. Pvt. Charles A. McCarthy, of the battalion's Company B, and another soldier captured three German machine guns, rushing one of them with no assistance. McCarthy and his fellow soldier then took twenty prisoners.[370] Lt. Walter V. Dial led "his platoon in attacking and destroying German machine gun nests." Despite incurring wounds, he continued to advance until being killed.[371] Though stricken with flu, Cptn. John P. Pryor stayed with his shorthanded unit, aiding it during heavy fighting around Exermont and Cote 240 until he physically collapsed on the battlefield. He died during his transport to the hospital.[372] First Lt. James G. Lusk reorganized the 2nd Machine Gun Battalion's remnants after all other officers had been killed or wounded. He led their attack, which captured six machine guns and imprisoned many enemy soldiers.[373]

The Americans established listening posts after dark in the ravine east of Cote 272. Bursts of German machine gun and extremely heavy howitzer fire, which the men called "whiz bangs," swept the area. American machine guns fired intermittently into enemy positions. Officers ordered survivors of the attack to dig in for the night and placed machine guns on the flanks. The assault and support companies exchanged positions after dark, with the stronger company supporting the weaker one. At the end of that day the assault had one commissioned officer, one non-commissioned officer and forty-seven privates left.[374] That night the entire 3rd Battalion could count three officers and 182 effectives. The battalion's total losses for the day were nine officers and 240 men killed and nine officers and 350 men wounded, over 50 percent casualties.[375]

Only one medic treated 120 wounded at the forward aid station on the northern edge of Cote 240, in the woods at the head of the little valley leading west toward the Ariétal Farm. While the walking wounded could typically get themselves out, the usual means of getting badly wounded casualties to the rear was using German prisoners under guard to carry them out on stretchers. No personnel was available to field-dress the walking wounded, and the battalion had no litter-bearers, so every wounded soldier feared abandonment. Because no one guarded the prisoners carrying stretchers to the rear, the arrangement was risky, but it helped wounded Americans receive treatment. However, reaching the aid station did not necessarily mean the wounded would survive—or even receive care, as the station's lone medic struggled to triage cases by himself. The aid station near Cote 240 became one of the 26th Infantry's most indelible tragedies, as over eighty soldiers died there.[376]

Back on the line, at midnight, the regimental commander authorized a detail of disciplined and experienced effectives to leave the line to help twenty-five walking wounded from the aid station back to the rear and to return with food. From experience, the officers knew that if they chose lesser men for this detail, as many as a third typically would not return, so the most trustworthy were picked. The detail made it back at 0400 with breakfast.

That night German General von Einem, commander of the Third Army, attributed the pause in the American attack to the "limited operative mobility of the Americans." He noted that the American Army could be expected to continue "to smash our front by increasing blows without regard to his losses" and added that "the enemy still has ample forces at his disposal for the continuation of the attacks."[377]

October 5 for the 1st Army

Summerall did not accomplish all he set out to do on October 5, but at the end of the day, he said, "the fighting was desperate on both sides and the losses heavy, the line was gained on schedule."[378] The Germans made a stubborn stand but were dislocated, and their best troops were outfought, though they continued to bring reinforcements.[379] The quality of 1st Division fighting for Cote 240 was of a high order. However, 1st Army results on both 1st Division flanks were disappointing, as the 4th Division on the left took three days to move a mile and the 32nd Division on the right did not reach its objective. The Americans buried seven hundred that day, and the division's medical units reported treating 5,050 men wounded or sick since the 1st Division operation started.[380]

While the day was not totally successful for the 1st Division, its artillery had been brilliant. Its infantry closely followed moving barrages as it passed over ground covered with 35th Division and German dead. The right brigade advanced two kilometers, and the left brigade advanced four kilometers. Summerall stated "This was the only spot on the Western Front where we gained the objective that day."[381]

Engineers hold and fight as infantry at Cote 269: October 5–9, 1918

While most of the 1st Division would continue advancing along Summerall's initial plan after October 5, one unit received an unusual, multi-day assignment that kept them somewhat separated from events elsewhere in the division. After Cote 269's capture by the 26th Infantry, its protection was turned over to the 32nd Division's infantry brigades operating on the 1st Division's right. Because of German positions directly in front of the point of liaison between the 1st and 32nd Divisions, both infantry brigades struggled to gain a foothold and suffered heavy casualties.[382]

To support the 32nd Division attack, the 1st Division ordered the last of its reserves, a battalion of the 1st Engineers at the Tronsol Farm, to join the fighting on Cote 269 as infantry. Commanded by Maj. Thomas F. Farrell, the engineers occupied the reverse slope of the hill and relieved the men from the 1st Division's 26th Infantry, who were on the hill's northeast slope, and two companies of the the entire hill, but he was killed before this was accomplished.[383] Cpl.

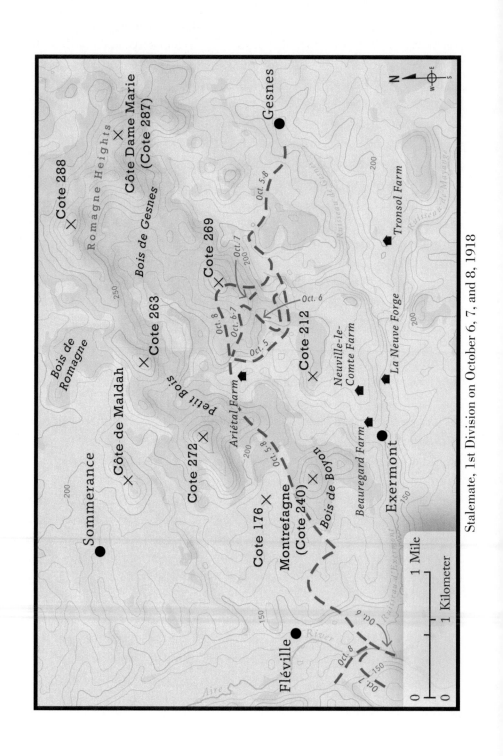

Stalemate, 1st Division on October 6, 7, and 8, 1918

John M. Gallagher, 1st Engineers, Company C, was positioned to receive an enemy counterattack and stayed at his post when the unit withdrew. Advancing, he discovered a German soldier stripping "the body of his dead commanding officer." Gallagher was later found supine with his rifle, surrounded by a circle of six dead Germans.[384]

At 1950 on October 6, Colonel Grant from 1st Army received a message from General Craig of I Corps, stating that Summerall's "men from 1st Division on Hill 269 have not been relieved." The message emphasized the many times that this information had been communicated, then noted, "General Summerall again requests that a staff officer if necessary come to his office and he will furnish that man with a guide to Hill 269 so that those from 1st Division may be relieved and that it be done promptly." The message underscored the severity of the situation by adding, "Casualties 1st Division 5,500 including everybody."[385]

Later that night, the 26th Infantry's two rifle companies that first secured the position were pulled off the hill but not out of the war. Orders put them back into the attack on Cote 272 with the 16th Infantry's 3rd Battalion.[386]

The 26th's Machine Gun Company was then ordered to reinforce the Engineers. On the night of October 8-9 it sent five guns, all that remained of the company's original twelve, to Cote 269.[387] In hand-to-hand fighting almost all the American machine gunners and a large number of the Germans were killed.[388]

Company A of the 1st Machine Gun Battalion reinforcing the engineers was ordered to stay on 269 for the next two days. On the morning of October 9, the surviving engineers were joined by elements of the battalion's Company B with eight machine guns. The officer commanding the newly arrived machine gunners said he was not under the orders of the engineers and that he had orders only to fire barrages. He refused to go forward and placed his guns under the two west knobs of Cote 269 while Germans occupied the top of the hill. The engineers then attacked the hilltop as infantry at 1830 on October 9. Ten-man parties went to the north and south slopes and succeeded in putting five men on the crest.

The engineers demonstrated numerous acts of bravery and courage on Cote 269. While commanding the troops holding the crest of Cote 269, 1st Lt. William Bourland was killed defending it a hundred yards ahead of his unit.[389] Pvt. Frank Lemaster stymied a counterattack by killing twelve of its participants with his rifle.[390] Single-handedly operating a machine gun against a superior force, Pvt. Kurt H. A. Koehler, an American soldier born in Germany, forced a retreat after killing a few enemy soldiers. Wounded and unable to continue manning the gun, he destroyed it with a pickaxe.[391] While leading his group on Cote 269, Sgt. 1st Class James E. Bracey and his men "came under direct machine gun fire. Bracey skillfully advanced his men" before individually capturing enemy gunner.[392] Pvt. Philip A. Daley volunteered twice to silence machine guns.[393]

Cpl. Leroy F. Marshall stalked a sniper by creeping three hundred yards across an area covered by machine gun fire. He killed the sniper and was himself killed.[394] Leading a patrol against a German machine gun, Sgt. James F. Tracy, Company B, led a patrol to an enemy machine gun and captured it, then continued to lead men forward until his death.[395] Cpl. David Thomas, Company A, twice advanced before his platoon, firing on enemy machine gunners until their deaths.[396] Another soldier in Company A, Russian-born Cpl. Anthony Savitsky, led his squad in surrounding multiple machine guns, silencing them, and capturing twenty Germans.[397] Cpl. Thomas Borkus, who was also born in Russia, along with another engineer serving as a rifleman, fired into the Germans, forcing them to retreat.[398] Cptn. Dan S. Helmick consolidated the friendly lines until wounded.[399]

The engineers fighting as infantry now held Cote 269 after a distinctive battle. Summerall asked for an investigation of the reinforcing machine gun officer who refused to obey the order issued by the engineers' commanding officer. He would be exonerated on October 14, 1918, by the Division Chief of Staff, who concluded that the machine gun officer had no intention of failing to cooperate with the senior engineering officer.[400]

Day Eleven: Sunday, October 6, 1918

Throughout October 6 1st Division soldiers mostly regrouped or held their position. However, some engaged in limited action. Pvt. Frank F. Dubord of the 28th Infantry Regiment volunteered as a point man and advanced four hundred yards ahead of his platoon until mortally wounded.[401] Pvt. Eugene M. Ashcraft also volunteered to go ahead of his unit through heavy fire to scout the enemy; he was able to convey German locations to his commander.[402] After having his wounds treated at the dressing station, Cpl. Roderick Evans, Company G, rejoined his platoon, leading it until he incurred an additional wound.[403]

The 26th Infantry Regiment's 3rd Battalion had corps permission to stay in place on October 6, but when an opportunity emerged, Frasier seized it. With Cote 269 secure, the battalion's skirmish line was consolidated and shortened. While the artillery moved its firing batteries forward, a friendly fog wrapped the bodies of the living and the dead.[404] When it cleared, Frasier saw enemy activity on Cote 272 from his position on Cote 212, and he decided to attack Cote 272. His adjoining units held steady, but his own position was weak when he asked for authority to attack.[405]

He received the permission at noon, and the attack jumped off at 1400. The 3rd Battalion then advanced to the base of 272 and drove the enemy from its position on the left flank of the hill's base. At about 1500 a German regiment formed for counterattack behind the Americans trying to get to Cote 272 in a valley running south from 212.

The 3rd Battalion attack came apart as German 77mm, minenwerfer (short-range mortars), and small arms wiped out entire platoons. The wounded accumulated too fast to be evacuated.[406] Such evacuations also posed risks, and Cpl. Neal D. Fenton, a medic with the 26th, was killed while trying to rescue a wounded soldier.[407] Demoralized by heavy fire, Company L retreated; Company M broke and ran. The entire battalion then went into the woods, and Frasier sent a runner to order Company K, still battered from its friendly fire event the previous day, to hold fast. It complied.

Frasier assessed the situation. Noting the company of Germans was behind his battalion, he decided to press on. Later he recalled his reasoning: "They outnumbered us three to one. There was but one thing to do. We had no support. We had no line of retreat. We had to attack them."[408]

The fleeing men steadied, turned around, and started shooting at the Germans, who were surprised by the small distance between the Americans. The men, who were standing side by side, gave the impression of being a larger force. The 3rd Battalion soldiers then fired from the shoulder, advancing rapidly while the Germans fled straight into fire from Company L's two machine guns. Frasier triumphantly recalled, "Then shells from the 7th Field Artillery began falling squarely in their midst."[409] Despite this progress, the Germans eventually pushed back, and the 3rd Battalion, for all its efforts, failed yet again to infiltrate Cote 272.

The food supply also failed again that night after the Regimental Commander, Col. Hjalmar Erickson, assured all three battalion commanders by telephone that a hot supper was on the way forward. After much heated conversation, concerning when the hungry men could expect food, the officer detailed to see that the food went forward and the three battalion commanders met with the regimental commander. The officers knew that men needed fresh food, both for nutrition and for morale. Speaking in somewhat broken English, the regimental commander said, "Dere is von officer here vot is a --- -- - -----. He vill at vonce get himself out of my PC." A member of the staff recalled, "That officer concerned with rations left and did not stop going until he was safe within the continental limits of the United States."[410]

Day Twelve: Monday, October 7, 1918

Adverse developments continued to stop the 1st Division, extending the previous day's relative stalemate. Cptn. Leonard R. Boyd recalled, "Every combat unit in the division, other than the 1st Battalion of the 16th Infantry which was still being held in reserve, had made at least one assault and received heavy casualties."[411] Still, the day's objectives were elusive across the entire front, and the division made no significant gains.

The 16th Infantry, less the "special reserve" detached 1st Battalion, remained in position at Fléville. It held on but could not advance, and no units moved to reinforce it. German airplanes dropped about sixty bombs on Fléville that afternoon.[412]

The 18th Infantry, on the forward slope of Cote 240, was unable to take the second objective of the day, Cote 176. The 28th Infantry, on the south of the Petit Bois, had failed to reach Cote 263 as planned.[413]

The 26th Infantry, slightly ahead of the 28th, was unable to take more than a piece of its second objective, Cote 272. The Germans were heavily gassing the positions on Cote 272, and the Americans units were preparing for an expected German counterattack. The 26th's 3rd Battalion was by then in the support position after merging with the depleted 1st Battalion; it was down to forty-three men and no officers. Americans took many prisoners that night, but in acknowledgement of the limited Americans available to guard prisoners, the regiment's orders were changed to exploit gains rather than taking prisoners.[414] Germans continued to put heavy artillery fire on the entire 26th Infantry.

Men of 18th Infantry, 1st Div., at first aid station being treated by Maj. W. A. Higgins under shell fire. Exermont Ardennes, France

Although the division failed to make measurable gains on October 7, at least one individual distinguished himself. The 26th's Sgt. Robert Blalock led a ten-man patrol against a strong enemy machine gun position. The citation for Blalock's Distinguished Service Cross described how he attacked the position "from the rear with admirable judgment. After expending all his ammunition, he continued the fight with two captured Luger pistols, and himself killed eight of the enemy in spite of being wounded." Thanks to the efforts of Blalock and his men, the nine thwarted machine gun nests yielded weapons that Americans used to defend the newly acquired position.[415] Blalock's service offered a rare bit of good news on a day that held little American progress.

Day Thirteen: Tuesday, October 8, 1918

The 1st Division stalemate continues

After failing in attacks on Cote 272 on October 5 and failing again on October 6, the 26th Infantry tried again at a different place on October 8 and was stopped again. At 0300 the enemy opened artillery fire into all 1st Division front lines, and the commander of the 26th ordered the 3rd and 1st Battalions to attack Cote 272 once more. The attack was initially planned for 0400 with two under-strength companies in the assault and two in support, but jump-off was postponed to 0500 due to heavy German machine gun fire. The attack went nowhere, even though that day and night the 6th Field Artillery pounded Cote 272 with fire.[416]

The 26th's 3rd Battalion had orders to advance again, but enemy infantry forming for an attack stopped the badly depleted unit. The 26th's 1st Battalion similarly failed to get anywhere attacking Cote 272 in another place—an effort followed by a German troop movement. Germans soundly stopped this, the 2nd Brigade's fifth advance on Cote 272. Three of the attacks had the sole object of taking that seemingly unattainable hill. The brave men continued to fight on during this discouraging day.[417]

Heavy incoming artillery fire threatened American troops from 1100 in the morning of October 8 until 1300. The battle went quiet that afternoon. At 1900 the 26th's 1st Battalion received the welcome word it would be relieved before daylight by the 28th Infantry's 2nd Battalion, which was due to arrive about 0330 on October 9.[418]

Casualties, including many officers, were mounting across the division. First Lt. Vance Mershon, 28th Infantry, assumed command of his battalion "after the battalion commander and all the senior officers had been killed or wounded," leading it until he was relieved after being wounded.[419] Cpl. Louis Dolce, a native of Italy who served with the 2nd Field Signal Battalion, volunteered to lay "a telephone line to an advanced observation post," which required moving approximately a half-mile through heavy fire, undergrowth, and barbed wire.[420] Sgt. John E. Personett, 16th Infantry, Company C, insisted on remaining in command of his platoon after being wounded. During an attack, all the group's other members also became casualties, but Personett, undaunted, single-handedly advanced on the platoon's objective, capturing the gun and crew.[421]

Doctors and medics also often rendered heroic service, working under dangerous conditions as they cared for wounded. Himself wounded, 1st Lt. Alfred M. Bergstein, a doctor attached to the 18th Infantry, refused evacuation until all other wounded soldiers received care.[422] A doctor born in Sweden, Cptn. Albert Linberg, 2nd Machine Gun Battalion, was also with the 18th Infantry when he crawled out of cover to amputate a wounded soldier's leg while exposed to sniping.[423]

The Germans took losses as well. Captured records revealed that the German 152nd Regiment's 3rd Company suffered a direct hit and was reduced to two platoons with one officer, three non-commissioned officers and twenty-eight men with two light machine guns.[424]

The 82nd Division makes a strategic gain on the 1st Division's eastern flank

Four days after the October 4 general attack, Maj. Gen. Hunter Liggett, commander of I Corps, solved the persistent problem behind much of the incoming German artillery and machine gun fire. Until then, the 1st Division's left flank and the 2nd and 3rd Battalions of its 16th Infantry at Fléville had been under fire from across the Aire Valley as Germans on the three-hundred-foot heights of Chatel-Chéhéry swept the ground in front of them with an enfilading fire without interruption.[425]

Liggett risked part of his corps reserve, several companies of Col. Frank Ely's 328th Infantry of the 82nd Division, ordering them across a rocky ford in the cold Aire River to get behind the Germans. Once in position in the 1st Division's sector they turned back to the east and drove against Germans on the high ground. An important strategic move, Liggett's plan was also a spectacular event viewed by the 16th Infantry soldiers across the river at Fléville. Liggett's imaginative and aggressive move helped break the initial resistance in the Argonne. Their objective was to cut off the German rail line near Cornay, but as part of this effort, they also rescued Maj. Charles Whittlesey's heroic "Lost Battalion" of the 77th Division, which had been cut off deep in the Argonne Forest since October 2. Whittlesey and 191 of the original 670 men from two battalions safely left their position.[426]

The German high command knew its position in the Argonne was untenable when the 82nd Division assaulted the Germans in the Chatel-Chéhéry Hills, cleaning out the machine gun nests one by one. It forced the Germans back, but they pressed forward again, only to be stopped from putting out the galling fire suffered for the previous six days and nights.

During the operation the 82nd Division's Cpl. Alvin York led sixteen men through strong German lines, where they killed an estimated twenty-eight men and took 132 prisoners.[427] This feat earned York a promotion to sergeant, and after the war he received the Medal of Honor. His story was immortalized by the 1941 Hollywood film *Sergeant York*. Like Whittlesey, York was an ordinary fighter in an ordinary division, not an elite soldier from a well-known unit. Whittlesey's division consisted mostly of draftees from New York City, while York's included draftees from the mountains of Tennessee.[428] When their stories became known, these events boosted the morale of the entire AEF and the folks at home.

During the month of October the AEF made a strategic decision that provided even more of a sense of winning and growing: it divided itself into two armies. As the AEF's Commander in Chief, General Pershing maintained overarching command of the armies, but he relinquished command of the 1st US Army, handing the reins to Liggett, and created a 2nd Army under Maj. Gen. Robert Lee Bullard. Both Liggett and Bullard were promoted to lieutenant general.[429]

Though the American mood was relatively optimistic, forces had a continuing need for more soldiers with experience. The military had a shortage of tested fighters, as large numbers of green troops were arriving from the United States and substantial casualties were suffered in the Argonne. Rifle Companies were reduced from 250 to 175 men, making it necessary to cannibalize some newly organized divisions for replacements just as those green units needed salting with experienced soldiers.[430] The flu also contributed to the shortage of men in the AEF. First Army doctors reported 150,000 cases in mid-October that filled both field and general hospitals. The Germans also suffered from the outbreak, tempering somewhat the number of Americans stymied by illness.[431] Still, disease offered just one more obstacle for the Americans, who still faced formidable challenges in the days ahead.

CHAPTER 4

The 1st Division resumes its offensive

Day Fourteen: Wednesday, October 9, 1918

The general attacks of September 26 and October 4 targeted Cote 272, and both failed. Every US division in the Argonne was assigned to the general attack on October 9, but taking Cote 272 was up to the 1st Division alone.[432] Practically all of the 1st Brigade assembled on the north slope of Cote 240 on the night of October 8, widening the front line from two miles to more than three.

Men across the division demonstrated courage and resilience throughout the day. Sgt. Edgar A. Runyan, Company A, 18th Infantry, "assumed command of his platoon after all other sergeants...had become casualties and led it through several successive attacks." Runyan suffered a head wound but resisted evacuation and "remained in command of the platoon until his company was relieved."[433] Lt. Bayard Brown, 26th Infantry, replaced his dead company commander and was killed fifty yards from the enemy position after reestablishing flanks and continuing the advance.[434] Sgt. Thaddeus Wilkinson, a medic with the 26th Infantry, incurred severe wounds while giving first aid to wounded soldiers under direct fire.[435] The 26th's 2nd Lt. Calvin D. Richards, along with seven machine gunners, though outnumbered, stopped a German attack after a hand-to-hand fight that included pistols and grenades. Despite losing four of his men, Richards held the position.[436] Second Lt. Marvin E. Stainton, a newcomer to the 1st Battalion's Company D, led a detachment into enemy territory, "capturing seven machine gun nests and forty-seven prisoners" before he was killed.[437]

The 16th Infantry's 1st Battalion is released from division reserve and moves to the point

When the October 4 advance began, the division commander set the 16th Infantry's 1st Battalion aside, rested and saved for a decisive need. The battalion was camped in a sheltered ravine near Charpentry on October 7 when it received orders to go cross-country that night for four miles in drizzling rain to an assembly point south of Exermont, where it met nearly two hundred men in the 16th's Machine Gun Company for the next day's attack. Together, they formed a task force of about a thousand men picked to capture Cote 272, which had survived five previous attacks without being captured.[438]

Officers took their first look at Cote 272 from Cote 240. Ration and water carts met the assembled attackers on the afternoon of October 8 at a clearing half a mile south of Cote 240, and troops received their first hot meal in thirty hours. That night they crossed the southernmost end of the Petit Bois at 2030 and dug in.

The 16th's 1st Battalion, first organized in Syracuse, New York, consisted of four rifle companies, three of which were formed in 1917. The fourth, Company D, was formed in July 1918 by transferring about thirty officers and men from the three original companies and adding about a hundred men from a replacement battalion.

On the night of October 8 one officer led thirty-five men in a back-up platoon of the 1st Machine Gun Battalion to the crest of Cote 240. Their orders were to fire across the valley at targets of opportunity on Cote 272 at the beginning of the attack the next morning. At jump-off time, however, enemy artillery blew up three of the team's machine guns, killing the platoon leader and killing or wounding all but five of the men.[439]

The division's sector ran along a line on the right from Cote 269 to the Tuilerie Farm, covering all of Cote 272.[440] To the left, the Fléville–Sommerance line bounded the 16th Infantry's 1st Battalion, which led the drive to the Tuilerie Farm. Getting the 1st Battalion and its Machine Gun Company to the jump-off position was complicated and time-consuming. The 3rd Platoon made the jump-off in time, while experiencing difficulties. Capt. Albert Helsley later recalled how the platoon looked for cover and concealment:

> In order to reach its position for the jump off the 3rd platoon had to follow in single file a little ravine for about 130 yards, then change direction to the right and a very steep slope, along a narrow path through a strip of exceedingly thick woods for three hundred yards and reform in a small open space…. At the designated time, the platoon commander, 3rd platoon moved out at the head of his platoon which was in a column of files about five paces between men. The fog was so heavy that he could not see beyond the fourth man in the column. …Upon reaching the ravine, he discovered he had only four men and learned the fifth and sixth men had been killed and the seventh man had lost his nerve and ducked into a shell hole. The men following thinking the platoon had been ordered to take cover had done so. The platoon leader took the 7th man out of the hole and started him up the path with the gun of one of the dead. The platoon was re-formed and moved forward without further trouble but 20 valuable minutes had been lost.[441]

The artillery plan to take Cote 272 included multiple zones of fire. It would employ all 1st Division Artillery to support discrete infantry operations coming one after the other. While some leaders might have diluted the artillery power to serve multiple operations at one time, General Summerall opted to use his hallmark strategy, the Summerall Barrage, concentrating artillery in one operation as part of a bigger battle, then using the same artillery pieces in a separate operation.[442] Describing this barrage on Cote 272, Summerall said, "I pounded that hill and everything in it, using all the guns of the Artillery Brigade."[443]

The 1st Battalion went into this, which would be its toughest battle, with about one-fourth of its men experienced from heavy combat at Cantigny and Soissons. All had participated in September's attack at St. Mihiel, a relatively minor action that offered a useful rehearsal, as it developed teamwork for the leap-frogging and passing-through that were used so successfully in the Argonne. The battalion's leadership also had experience; twelve of the battalion's sixteen officers had commanded their units in at least one previous battle.[444]

Communication systems were readied, and telephone communications were better than at any time so far in the Argonne actions. Effective visual signal stations were installed on Cotes 240 and 269. Still, Cote 272 was by far the most formidable German position in the approach to the Côte de Châtillon, Cote 260.[445] The US kept up heavy artillery fire on it all night October 8.

Everybody knew the importance of this make-or-break attack. In addition to supporting artillery and the assault force of a thousand men, four groups of machine guns controlled by the division's machine gun officer participated. Each group had one company with twelve guns and was ordered to fire a standing barrage for ten minutes in front of the first objective. The 2nd Machine Gun Battalion provided seventy carts for moving the ammunition—twenty thousand rounds per gun. Once the battle got under way the carts would be used to bring forward ammunition for riflemen and to evacuate seriously wounded.[446]

The 16th Infantry's 1st Battalion passes through the 28th Infantry on Cote 272

Starting at 0500 on the morning of October 9, the Machine Gun Battalion put indirect fire into the enemy defenses. Both the American and German artillery started firing before the battle began. At 0830 the 16th Infantry assault battalion and its machine gunners— companies B and C, with A and D in support—formed in dense fog in the woods where they spent the night.

The complicated artillery plan began with a barrage by all corps and division artillery prior to the attack. Twenty-two minutes later, its fire shifted to a dense rolling barrage in front of the 2nd Brigade attacking Cote 263. The few surviving members of the platoon from

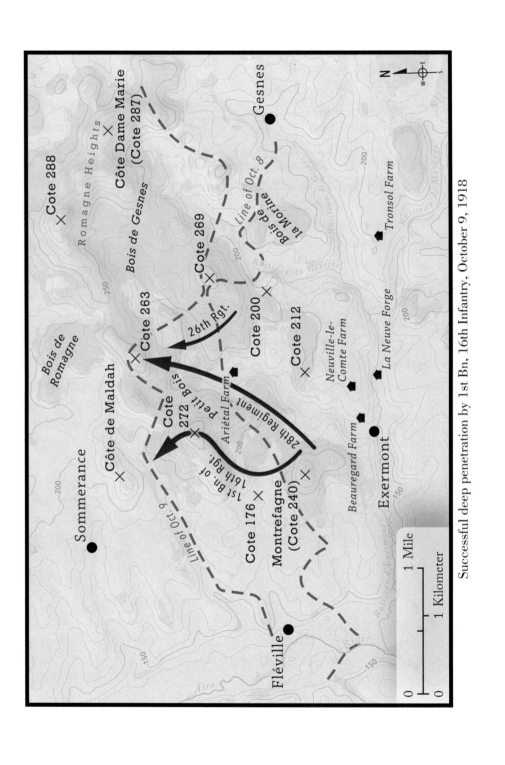

Successful deep penetration by 1st Bn, 16th Infantry, October 9, 1918

the 16th Machine Gun Company on Cote 240, commanded by Cpl. Fred O. Benning, supported the attack by firing on Cote 272 until they again came under heavy German artillery fire.[447]

The 1st Brigade was to advance to the new line and wait for two hours while the guns hit the next objective. Then, at H plus three hours a new rolling barrage would lead the 2nd Brigade forward to its second objective. In that attack, all divisional guns would lead the 1st Battalion's assault element forward again at H plus 290 minutes. For its final assault on Cote 272 all the division artillery was to deliver another massed rolling barrage in support of the attack battalion.

For the third attack, preceded by another thirty-minute massed artillery preparation and dense rolling barrage, the remainder of the 1st Brigade on the far left would drive forward to the second objective. Prior to the infantry jump-off, which included a rolling barrage, the artillery fired on German positions. The barrages moved very slowly—just one hundred meters every six minutes.[448]

Much of this elaborate plan did not work, as is often the case in battle. Fog disrupted the timing, which was also affected when the first rolling barrage went beyond the assaulting infantry's hearing. Still, scientific analysis after the action ranked this plan as demonstrating top utilization of concentrative fire in the tactical employment of field artillery.[449]

Dense fog limited visibility at the time of jump-off to fewer than twenty-five yards. Company commanders scrambled to find their flanking units. However, the fog carried a benefit for the Americans, who could not be seen by the German gunners using direct-fire 77s and machine guns from Cote 272.

At jump-off all four of the 16th Infantry's attacking companies and attached machine gunners were to pass through the 28th Infantry's infantrymen in place at the northern foot of Cote 240. Though the 28th's soldiers had orders to stand fast until the 16th Infantry's assault units passed through their lines, some 28th men panicked and started running to the rear when they saw the 16th coming forward through the fog. Officers restored order quickly, supported by passing word for them to stop and by the regiment's general belief that men running to the rear could be shot first and questioned later. The fog started to break up, and casualties increased. German machine guns swept the plain as the 1st Battalion advanced.[450]

Due to the fog, the assault and support companies could not see each other or help each other with directions. Company B's commanding officer led his men forward by using a compass. As the attack got underway, neither the battalion commander nor other companies knew Company B's location. The division history described, "With a dash that was worthy of its mission, the 1st Battalion, 16th Infantry then crossed the valley and reached the base of Hill 272."[451] This was accomplished while every company leap-frogged the one ahead of it, and all struggled to maintain a proper position relative to the first wave.[452]

Two platoons of the Machine Gun Company assigned to the assault battalion were behind the four rifle companies. They advanced by bounds with their guns while staying three or four hundred yards behind the infantry. These men were tired nearly to exhaustion from the physical and mental strain of dragging the guns, which weighed nearly twenty-three pounds, forward up the steep hills.[453] The machine gun platoon lieutenants on the assault line with the infantry picked out firing positions. Each squad took its gun to its place and began to dig an emplacement.[454]

The men surveyed the area, noting its terrain. Cptn. Leonard R. Boyd recalled, "Small, irregular patches of woods were scattered over the hill except for the southern slope that was barren. The ground swelled gently to the base of the Cote 272 then broke off in a steep, difficult climb."[455]

The fog remained unpredictable. It covered Cote 272 at the jump-off line, but as it cleared the Germans scattered fire over the valley. Heavy machine gun fire from the left of the battalion hit the Company C commander, most of the non-commissioned officers, and many privates. Officers placed survivors into a single platoon, commanded by a sergeant.

The attacking infantry took fire from the slopes ahead and from the left rear until the soldiers stopped in a swale in front of Cote 272 and reorganized. On reaching the base of 272 they continued up the hill's first rise.[456] The rolling artillery barrage outdistanced them then. Slowed by fog, men were so far behind the barrage at the foot of the hill that they could not even hear the artillery barrage they were supposed to follow.

The Germans opened fire when the attacking Americans headed up the steep part of 272. The 1st Division history recalled, "Thickets near its base were full of machine guns and mortars sited to cover every avenue of approach. The men crept up the steep slopes, and casualties continued to mount."[457] Men pulled each other up or pulled themselves by holding on to shrubs or small trees. With spotty visibility, they might see for 150 or 200 yards, then only fifty or sixty yards, sometimes fewer. More troops came under fire as the morning wore on and fog thinned. They continued to advance, running across small islands of good visibility and stopping to catch a breath in places covered by fog.

As the men advanced closer to German positions, messengers provided the only communication between companies and between the companies and battalion. The battalion commander, after losing all his messengers to fire or being unable to locate them in the fog, finally located Company D and ordered it to move abreast of Company B in the assault wave.[458]

Artillery fire, machine gun bullets, and minenwerfer shells seemed to be coming at the attackers from all directions, hitting men every few minutes and causing frequent halts. A deluge of fire fell on the attackers; many were killed, including the company commander and a platoon leader of the Machine Gun Company attacking with the infantry.[459] Enemy machine guns fired at close range, causing several hundred casualties. Everybody could see what was happening, but the attack did not let up. The German defenses were well organized.[460]

Capturing German machine guns in the fog became a matter of flanking a position and taking it. A company commander would order out one or two squads, whose men would leave their lines and disappear into the fog. The patrol would then return with the gun and sometimes with one or more prisoners to be sent to the rear. Taking prisoners was easy, but that was not the overall mission, and all the men were conditioned to continue to the objective.[461] Depending on the leader's preference, Americans either sent the German gunners to the rear or to their maker. When the men coming back reported no machine guns to the immediate front, the lines moved forward.[462] A good machine gunner would aim at the ankles of enemy soldiers, causing the falling bodies to become riddled with bullets.

Infantry patrols went out with orders to bring in as many prisoners as possible, and the Germans close by offered little resistance.[463] However, most 1st Battalion men went forward to the objective rather than losing time to take prisoners, as that was a far safer job. Everybody knew that casualties were reduced by moving fast.[464] Officers believed they should keep going forward while the going was good.

Fire coming down from the distant Côte de Maldah continued to cost 1st Battalion casualties.[465] A dominant terrain feature, the Côte de Maldah lay about a thousand yards from Cote 272 and rose 240 meters above the plain. As intermittent enemy fire appeared throughout the advance up Cote 272, few of the Americans remained in recognizable groups. Everything depended on individual initiative and small unit operations.[466]

By then the Machine Gun Company had only four guns and twenty men left of its initial twelve guns and three platoons. Its commanding officer was dead, killed while leading the group to protect the battalion Post of Command (PC). A platoon sergeant took over. With no time to set up the guns, he pulled out his automatic pistol and started firing at Germans sixty-five or seventy yards away, quite a distance for a .45. His men joined in the firing. When the firing stopped the group counted two German officers killed and twenty-seven German enlisted men killed or wounded in the three- or four-minute exchange. After reorganizing into two squads, the sergeant took two machine guns with as much ammunition as they could carry and continued up the slope towards the top of Cote 272. On the way, they ran into 3rd Platoon survivors with a machine gun. By the time they got to the top of the hill, the group had eighteen or twenty men armed with three guns and 3,500 rounds of ammunition.

The sergeant brought the handful of men into action on top of the hill, firing effectively into groups of Germans 1,200 to 1,500 meters away on Côte de Maldah.[467] Patrols then went into the woods beyond the top of Cote 272 and brought in prisoners. They offered no resistance, and one provided details of a planned counterattack.

Despite such successes, the battle was taking a heavy toll on the men. After all other members of his squad had been killed, PFC Alick Carrole, 16th Infantry, Company D, single-handedly killed two machine gunners and captured six men.[468] Pvt. George Van Buren, Company L, showed similar endurance when he fainted after being seriously wounded; on recovering consciousness, he rejoined the battle and helped stop the expected counterattack before taking a fourth wound and being evacuated.[469]

Many officers were casualties during these attacks. The 18th Infantry's Maj. John G. Emery led a battalion through fog until he was severely wounded.[470] Cptn. Harry L. Kimmell, 16th Infantry, was killed leading his rifle company in an advance.[471] First Lieutenant Helsley led part of his machine gun platoon in "capturing the enemy's strong point and relieving an exposed flank from heavy fire."[472] Second Lt. Wilson Brown Dodson, Company A, was killed leading his platoon. An outstanding combat officer, he was earlier mentioned three times in division orders for gallantry.[473] Cptn. August F. Behrendt led three assaults against machine guns firing point-blank into his troops. In one assault, he captured a machine gun and its crew after half his men had been killed or wounded.[474] Cpl. Frank Zilkey pressed forward alone after all his squad became casualties. He captured one machine gun and crew; he was killed while going after another.[475] Sgt. James E. Porter, Company C, attacked the enemy machine gun with four other soldiers, capturing the gun though "all his men were either killed or wounded" during the assault.[476] Sgt. George Petrimean, Machine Gun Company, 16th Infantry, was killed while guiding his section through heavy fire "to engage an enemy machine gun."[477]

Many acts of bravery and service beyond the call of duty were accomplished by wounded men. Cpl. Hyman Yarnis, Russian born, volunteered to attack a machine gun enfilading the lines with fire.

He killed the crew, incurred wounds, advanced against another machine gun, and continued attacking the enemy crew despite receiving additional wounds.[478] Sgt. Charlie E. Lemmon, Company M, 16th Infantry, working alone and incurring serious wounds, captured a machine gun and enabled his company's advance.[479] The 16th Infantry's Cpl. Ralph Ball, badly wounded, guided his section through a barrage and to safety before agreeing to evacuation.[480] Another soldier, James W. Barkalow, 18th Infantry, Company C, assembled seven men. Together, they captured a machine gun while taking a prisoner and killing a soldier. Moving on, they captured thirty-five more men, sent them to the rear, and captured five more while under fire.[481]

Despite the considerable shooting by both sides on the ground, the skies were rather peaceful. German airplanes flew throughout the 1st Battalion's occupation of Cote 272, but they were not hindered by Allied aircraft.[482]

Still, hard fighting continued, particularly for men in the 16th Infantry. With four members of his automatic rifle squad wounded, Cpl. Earl S. Noble, in the 16th's assault element, silenced a "machine gun just as another enemy machine gun on the flank opened fire and killed him."[483] Pvt. Arthur S. Long of Company D, along with an automatic rifleman, advanced against a 77mm gun position and captured its crew.[484] With a fellow soldier, Cpl. William B. Main, "advanced on a German 77mm gun," forcing its crew to withdraw.[485] Pvt. Herman Wallenmaier, Company D, wounded, remained with his company until his superiors commanded him to leave for treatment.[486]

After four trying days, the Americans succeeded in taking Cote 272 on October 9. Companies advanced piecemeal, rather than as units, but it worked because of the fog's concealment.[487] Amazingly, at about 1100 elements of all companies arrived at the top of the hill in order: Companies D, C, A, and B.[488] About half of those at the beginning of the attack were present at the end, along with seven officers. They rested and enjoyed the scenery until 1330, when American artillery then delivered heavy fire in front of the 16th Infantry with a barrage that led it over the top of Hill 272.

The battalion commander sent a platoon from Company D to the left of 272, where they saw Germans in small groups willing to surrender. Pvt. Elvid B. Johnson, a medic with 2nd Machine Gun Battalion, reported that prisoners were out of food and hungry.[489]

By early afternoon the division had, for the first time in the Meuse-Argonne, taken all its objectives. It had captured more than six hundred prisoners and advanced the line.[490] As the fog cleared, the 18th Infantry could be seen two hundred yards to the rear of the assault battalion, the 16th's 1st Battalion.

The enemy could also see well and continued to make futile attempts to hold portions of the hill.[491] Machine gun and rifle fire came in from the left front but without much effect. This time there was no counterattack. Instead there was more artillery causing many casualties that could not be treated. The battalion commander ordered a retreat to the ravine on the right side and north of the foot of the hill, where a skirmish line dug in.[492]

At sunset two American planes used hand signals to ask for the front-line position of the 1st Battalion and waved a friendly greeting. The gesture offered the soldiers welcome proof that they were not forgotten at a time when Germans were on both flanks and in front. The soldiers gained comfort from believing their position would be reported immediately to division headquarters. They likely also appreciated news from men coming in with water from a spring in the woods, as they reported seeing hundreds of Germans trying to surrender.

Just before dark, soldiers finally established a telephone connection with the 18th Infantry's regimental headquarters. Because the 16th Infantry was still on point, it had no connection with the division commander. After German wire was spliced to extend the American telephone communication for over five hundred yards to connect the 18th's headquarters and the 16th Infantry, another important link was made, and the 18th transmitted the 16th's orders.[493] Twice during this operation 2nd Lt. Maurice S. Stevenson worked as a messenger and exposed himself to fierce artillery and machine gun barrages while transporting the brigade commander's orders to the assaulting 1st Battalion. Though he was wounded, he completed his mission before accepting evacuation for treatment.[494] As the division wrapped up a day of progress, it used the new telephone connection between battalion and regiment, ordering each regiment, including the 16th, to push out patrols at 0700 on the following morning in its sector, moving forward and exploiting gains.[495]

In reviewing the results of his corps, Summerall recalled the battle to take Hill 272 as "one of the hardest fought actions of the war."[496] Many units suffered significant losses; for example, the Machine Gun Company accompanying the 16th Infantry would lose all of its officers and 75 percent of the men not in the command section.[497]

Still, the 1st Division had accomplished a great deal. It held the area from Fléville to Hill 269.[498] And when the 16th's 1st Battalion completed its advance through Hill 272, it cleared the way for the its 2nd Brigade to join the 1st Brigade in advancing to the overall corps objective: the heavily fortified Côte de Châtillon.[499]

Day Fifteen: Thursday, October 10, 1918

The 16th Infantry's 1st Battalion moves to take Côte de Maldah

General Summerall ordered his troops to exploit successes, which meant they were to probe until hitting resistance, then stop. The 1st Division was to make no more massive attacks, though its 1st Battalion's final objective was to take a German barracks located on the Côte de Maldah, the next hill beyond Hill 272. At 0700 on October 10, Company D and the remaining platoon-sized force from Company C moved to the top of Côte de Maldah. Because one-fourth of the men in Company D, all excellent fighters, were foreign-born, the unit was referred to by other companies as "The Foreign Legion." The men dug in on the reverse slope while taking German machine gun fire and flat trajectory 77mm fire from Germans sharing the hill with them.

The sergeant commanding Machine Gun Company brought it into action on top of the hill, firing into groups of Germans 1,200 to

1,500 meters away on Côte de Maldah.[500] Patrols went into the woods beyond the top of Cote 272, and they brought back prisoners offering no resistance, one of whom told of a planned counterattack.

The opposing forces on Côte de Maldah and Cote 272 continued firing back and forth. Patches of small trees provided camouflage to the 1st Battalion's firing positions on the Côte de Maldah, from which they fired at the remnant of Germans on Hill 272. Its north slope and wooded ravine were all highly visible from the Côte de Maldah.[501] Men from the 16th Infantry on the Côte de Maldah crawled up a ravine and outflanked the Germans on Hill 272, capturing three cannons. About 150 Germans armed with machine guns attacked the Côte de Maldah, but the 16th pushed them back. Another unsuccessful German attack followed.

American officers ordered some men to go out and kill enemy snipers who were making it dangerous to move around. All but one returned to the lines, causing everyone on the position to feel safer with regard to the snipers. On the other hand, German artillery fire caused so many casualties they could not be cared for, forcing the American commander to retreat to a ravine in the rear, which would become the battalion's new front line. The 1st Battalion's last remnants, five officers and fewer than two hundred men, were thrown together there. As night fell, they dug in, set up a perimeter of defense, and placed squads out as guards.

Two officers wounded at the Côte de Maldah headed to the rear on foot, collecting two German officers and about eighty men as prisoners along the way. They put the prisoners into a column with one American officer at the head and one at the rear. American leadership expected any wounded Americans going to the aid station to bring in Germans collected along the way.[502]

The 28th Infantry relieves the 16th Infantry's 1st Battalion and takes Hill 263

Early on the night of October 9, the 28th Infantry's 2nd Battalion received orders to relieve the 16th Infantry's 1st Battalion. The change of command took place on the morning of October 10, after which the 16th's 1st Battalion moved into the Bois de Moncy to take up a support position behind the 26th Infantry, which stood at the sector's right flank. During this move, the battalion captured a German patrol in a complicated and difficult flanking move performed by a large body of totally worn-out American soldiers.[503]

The 28th Infantry was commanded by Maj. Clarence R. Huebner, whose six-year service as an enlisted man in the 1st Division preceded his receiving a direct commission on November 26, 1916. As a company commander at Cantigny, he was promoted to major and replaced his mortally wounded battalion commander. After commanding a battalion early in the Argonne battles, he was promoted to command the 28th Infantry Regiment.[504]

Before further advance, the 28th and 26th Regiments completed a necessary shift to the right in order to straighten the line. The 28th Infantry then crossed the ravine in front of the Ariétal Farm, a position on the south side of le Petit Bois that put its 1st Battalion in position to attack Hill 263 with 419 men, which it did.

The 28th came under a rain of German artillery shells but was helped out of the situation by American artillery. By then the 1st Division held Cotes 240 and 212, offering an opportunity for its artillery to adjust fire from them.

The 28th's 2nd Battalion jumped off behind a rolling barrage fired from Cote 240 at 0830. Morning fog saved the advance from being seen by Germans but made it hard for the assault wave to find flanking units. Four guns from the regimental Machine Gun Company, scattered throughout the regiment, supported the attack. The 3rd Battalion helped from its position about three hundred yards ahead, and fifty more machine guns put indirect fire on Hill 263 by shooting over the heads of the attackers.

The valley in front of Cote 263 was completely covered by German artillery fire from Cote 272, which was still occupied by both Germans and Americans. The concealing fog did not last long, and the 28th Infantry's advance halted after about two hundred yards. The 2nd Battalion took a position to cover the forward slope and the valley, after which German machine guns hit them.[505]

Hill 263 was so steep in some places that men had to grasp bushes to help pull themselves up while climbing.[506] Company M outflanked a German machine gun holding up the advance but was nearly annihilated by German artillery hitting it at the same time. Concussion knocked soldiers unconscious. An observer recalled, "It seemed the enemy was using up all his heavy artillery ammunition . . . an entire squad would be blown from the face of the earth."[507]

Troops advanced slowly up Cote 263. The 28th's 3rd Battalion passed through its 1st Battalion, which used all three battalions of the 28th Infantry in the advance. By noon the assaulting 3rd Battalion was halfway up Cote 263, accompanied by a 37mm gun pulled by three men and joined by two men carrying ammunition.

The commander of the 28th Infantry's support battalion reached the assault battalion at about 1500, just as it cleared the crest of Cote 263. To the front lay the long open stretch between Cote 263 and Landres-et-Saint-Georges. He saw three batteries of German artillery in full flight along with two machine gun companies and three infantry battalions.[508]

The 6th Field Artillery caught and dispersed an enemy force getting ready to counterattack 263. The Germans continued to be driven back, though they blew out telephone lines as quickly as Americans put them down. The 28th's 1st Battalion dug in on Cote 263's southwestern slope and moved down its north slope, completely clearing the hill of enemy troops.[509]

Serious sniping on the 28th began as the 26th's 2nd and 3rd Battalions also descended the forward slope. Both regiments were so weakened that their point battalions joined. By actual count the eighty-five men of the 26th's 3rd Battalion carried sixty-three automatic rifles in addition to their Springfield rifles, which held a clip of four rounds. A German barrage soon reduced the eighty-five men to about seventy.[510]

The whole 1st Division advanced about a mile that day by sending patrols out and having soldiers follow them into unoccupied territory.[511] There was no serious resistance, as the enemy appeared to have given up on any idea of more fighting until safely behind the hardened fortifications of the Kriemhilde Stellung. Summerall regarded that position as too strong for his division and made no attack on it.[512]

The 28th's 1st Battalion then dug in on the southwestern slope of Cote 263. Meanwhile, several instances of subordination appeared in the sector. Some men in the 28th's 3rd Battalion resisted when ordered to continue the attack. Company K, commanded by a sergeant, retreated. The battalion commander stopped part of the company, but the remainder continued to the rear and was not brought under control until the battle ended.[513]

Troops from another unit, called a pioneer outfit, also demonstrated insubordination. Pioneer platoons belonged to the Corps of Engineers and performed demolition or construction work. In this case, when the platoon was sent forward to evacuate 28th Infantry wounded lying on stretchers exposed to shellfire, the 1st Lieutenant in charge objected to letting his men come under such fire.[514]

The 1st Division resumed its advance that afternoon, taking about 230 German prisoners. German resistance was diminishing, but German artillery continued to throw gas shells into American positions. The forward slope of Côte de Maldah, still held by the 16th's 1st Battalion, was heavily shelled in the afternoon, and German airplanes flew over the hill, dropping small bombs.[515]

Many men in the 28th remained valiant in the challenging circumstances. During the advance, Pvt. Dale W. Lloyd of infantry headquarters set up and manned an observation post while wounded.[516] Pvt. Frank D. Miller served the 28th's Medical Detachment even when its staff consisted of only two other men.[517]

Of course, other units also had heroic men. Pvt. Eddie J. Parent of the 26th Infantry's Company G, "crawled forward and silenced a machine gun" without assistance.[518] The 16th Infantry's battalion commander sent out a three-man patrol and lost two of them, the price it took to learn that his men were the lone Americans on the point. At 1310 he reported that the 18th's 2nd Battalion was never brought even with him on the front. Enemy machine gun fire stopped PFC Gottlieb Luzow's advancing platoon. With another man, Luzow put the gun out of action, and the advance was continued.[519] Cpl. George Nelson of the 18th Infantry's Company A went in front of the line and captured a machine gun and crew.[520]

Every regiment routinely pushed out patrols in its sector, moving forward and exploiting gains.[521]

That night on the Côte de Maldah's eastern slope, Americans captured a rolling kitchen, which the hungry and exhausted soldiers received gratefully. As the evening wore on, 6th Field Artillery pounded Germans who were still on Cote 272.[522] Captured German records revealed confusion in its 54th Division, reporting a "lack of ammunition and failure of reinforcements."[523] This report confirmed something some of the men had already started to observe in certain moments, such as when Italian-born Pvt. Petro Ruggero, working alone, "charged an enemy machine gun, killing the operator and capturing the gun."[524] The battalion scout officer reported no resistance in front of him.[525]

The 1st Division advanced about 4.32 miles from October 4 to October 10 while both flanks and its front were exposed to enemy fire throughout the effort.[526] In that week the division suffered 7,500 casualties—1,594 killed and 5,834 wounded. In the three days before the October 4 attack, it had about 1,500 casualties, making for the heaviest losses of any division in the Meuse-Argonne campaign.[527] Division Headquarters would later account for 1st Division casualties as 8,969 killed, wounded, and missing in the Meuse-Argonne.[528]

Day Sixteen: Friday, October 11, 1918

The end of the 1st Division's fighting in the Argonne

Germans throughout the Kriemhilde Stellung supported the Côte de Châtillon with well-organized fire.[529] German artillery fired on all movement of the 16th Infantry's 1st Battalion as it made its last advance by running down the forward slope of the Côte de Maldah. There it captured a German colonel, who said he "had been cut off by the barrage on October 9 and was unable to move from his dugout."[530] Soldiers from the 16th saw the 18th Infantry coming up at a distance on their left and to the rear. They dug in at 1600 with two machine guns to cover the two-thousand-yard gap between the two regiments.[531] By nightfall the regiments were side by side, but they were still separated by the gap, which ran along the northern edge of Bois de Romagne, the wood surrounding the village of Romagne, which was incorporated into the German Hindenburg Line.[532] Patrols went out on October 11, probing and waiting for the other infantry battalions to draw even.[533]

When patrols went out, they successfully took prisoners and silenced and captured guns. Pvt. Thomas F. Price led four men against an enemy machine gun nest and silenced the gun.[534] Sgt. Homer Purcell, 16th Infantry, Company B, led men who "surrounded a heavy trench mortar...defended by two machine guns." He shot the non-commissioned officer who was commanding, then imprisoned members of the crew.[535]

Sgt. Mack O. Oliver, 28th Infantry, Company H, knowing his company to be dangerously short of men, refused to leave the line despite being seriously wounded.[536] First Lt. Harry Sprague Silver "led a patrol...to establish liaison with the units on the left flank," continuing until forced back by heavy casualties but returning with critical intelligence to share with his battalion commander.[537]

Despite the 1st Division's advances, it had not captured its primary objective, the Côte de Châtillon. The division had suffered substantial casualties, and soon its Argonne war would become somebody else's responsibility. The 42nd Rainbow Division's relief of the 1st Division began that night when the 42nd's advance parties entered the sector. Command was to pass at 0800 hours on October 12, the next day. The Big Red One had fought its last significant battle of the war and was proud to be one of the finest units in the AEF, probably the finest, as it enjoyed the reputation of being Pershing's favorite. The 1st Division had fought hard and suffered oppressive casualties against the German strongholds, but its men had failed to reach and eliminate the final and most important stronghold: the Kriemhilde Stellung.[538]

Nonetheless, in an official account the division history said, "This assault must ever stand as one of the most brilliant exploits of the Division."[539] Its legendary assault unit, the 16th Infantry's 1st Battalion, suffered ten officers and nearly four hundred enlisted men killed or wounded between October 9 and October 11.[540] By the start of October 12, when the relief was complete, the point company had shrunk to sixty-eight men and two officers, one of whom was wounded.[541] In closing out its part of the 1st Brigade battle, the 18th Infantry reported 8 officers and 332 men present, having lost 38 officers and 1,384 men killed, wounded or missing. Not one of the officers who entered the battle with the regiment on October 1 would come out of it with the unit when it was relieved on October 11; all had died or been evacuated.

There were no serious incidents during the relief. No trucks were available to the 1st Division when the command changed, so the men started the seventy-five-kilometer trip to the rear on foot.[542] The 16th Infantry began moving over the captured ground near Cheppy, often encountering wounded along the way. Pvt. Donald Kyler recorded his impressions:

> We found a wounded man who had been shot in the back five days before. How he survived without any care I do not know. I observed that sometimes a man who apparently was not badly wounded would promptly die. Others, badly shot up would not only survive but would recover and live for years. A case of that kind was a man whom I bound up and helped to carry to an aid station. A shell fragment had entered his foot. His leg was bent back with bone protruding. One hand was badly cut, and a slit was cut in his forehead with the bone showing. Years later he wrote me that he was alright except for a short leg and a malfunctioning hand.[543]

The biggest relief for the soldiers might have been a hot meal on the morning of the relief; for some it was only the second or third in six days. Every man was issued a blanket and a shelter-half, a ground sheet he could use for sleeping upon or, when combining with others, for making a pup tent. Badly bedraggled and worn out, none of the men had shaved for two weeks, though they had lost track of the date and even the day of the week. Many could barely speak above a whisper due to gas acting on vocal chords. They could distinguish daylight from dark, but little else.

Kyler summed up his part succinctly:

> I was tired physically and mentally. I had seen mercy killings, both of our hopelessly wounded and those of the enemy. I had seen the murder of prisoners of war singly and as many as several at one time. I had seen men rob the dead of money and valuables and had seen men cut off the fingers of corpses to get rings. Those things I had seen but they did not affect me much. I was too numb. To me corpses were nothing but carrion. I had the determination to go on performing as I had been trained to do - - to be a good soldier.[544]

In the changeover, Summerall ordered the 1st Division's 1st Field Artillery Brigade and its ammunition train to stay in place to support the next V Corps attack. The 1st Division captured 1,407 prisoners in October. While many of those Germans were defeated and willing to surrender, it was still a brilliant exploit.[545]

Pershing would later praise the 1st Division in General Order 201, dated November 19, 1918, the only AEF order of commendation that cited a single division.[546] In his foreword to the *History of the First Division*, he remembered their service:

> It is particularly gratifying to me to have the opportunity of writing a foreword for the History of this splendid Division. Your organization landed in France as the advance guard of America's fighting men. You were the first to confront the enemy and the first to attack him. You established the reputation of the American Soldier in Europe, and you have maintained our ideals by the dignity and self-restraint of your bearing on German soil. The record of your accomplishments and your sacrifices will be a model for our armies in the future.[547]

Of all the sectors on the Western Front, this was the most important to the Germans.[548] Although the 1st Division was finished, hard fighting continued, and casualties mounted. As the 42nd Division assumed its position, rumors circulated of a forthcoming German offer to accept President Wilson's "Fourteen Points" for ending the war. A German communique, sent through the Swiss government and requesting negotiations for an armistice, reached the White House.[549]

However, Wilson declined the request in a short and curt message to the Germans.[550]

At this critical moment, the US Army-wide offensive appeared to be stopped, and "all units were ordered in an official way to hold the ground gained from one of the most determined advances in the history of warfare."[551] Still, it was unlikely they would simply hold forever. The AEF numbered nearly two million men by then, with more Americans than British on the Allied front in France.[552] In time, those men, including soldiers in the 42nd Division, would see dramatic action.

CHAPTER 5

The 42nd Division replaces the 1st Division

Summerall assumes command of V Corps

At Liggett's suggestion, General Pershing promoted General Summerall from command of the 1st Division to command of V Corps, insuring seamless continuity in the fight for the Côte de Châtillon.[553] The 1st Division had been under Summerall, one of Pershing's most experienced and successful combat generals, in the battle for that hill since September 30, and some credit Summerall's promotion to the Summerall Barrage, his successful system of concentrating artillery fire.[554] Pershing had high expectations for the artillery expert when he ordered him to capture the Côte de Châtillon, "the most elaborate defensive system on the Western Front."[555]

It was no coincidence that the V Corps included the 42nd Division, a National Guard division with a strong reputation for hard fighting. Summerall knew the Rainbow well, having commanded all its artillery when the division was organized at Camp Mills, New York, in 1917.[556] As V Corps commander, he would approve the 42nd's attack plan. Though no other division had successfully taken the Côte de Châtillon, officials held great hopes for the 42nd.

42nd Rainbow Division moves to the Front

The Rainbow Division's hardest test and most important strategic operation was ahead. The division carried the main burden in attacking the Côte de Châtillon.[557] Its four infantry regiments—the 165th (New York), the 166th (Ohio), the 167th (Alabama), and the 168th (Iowa)—would each take part in the coming attack.

The division had traveled from St. Mihiel, arriving on October 5 and waiting for several days in the overcrowded and shot-up forests near Verdun. Shell holes from past battles were everywhere, and drivers of wagons or trucks stuck carefully to the roads, knowing they could not make it through otherwise. Men received overcoats and blankets as the weather grew colder.[558]

Experienced combat soldiers understood that simply bringing the division together at the front was a big and complicated operation, and the situation was getting harder and more dangerous. A number of American observation balloons hovered nearby and were attacked by German planes.[559] Several American balloons caught fire, forcing artillery observers to use their parachutes. German aviators sprayed thousands of bullets into camps and dropped propaganda leaflets.

Some units took a week to get into attack positions, as conditions were terrible. It was hard to even partially dry out, and there was no place to sleep other than on the ground in the open. During the long nights the only way to keep warm was to roll up in a blanket with all of your clothes on. But waiting at least provided an opportunity to stop, wash clothes, and pick out the "cooties," the soldiers' term for lice. Although the potable water point was nearly a mile away, it had been more than a month since they had hot water and a place to delouse clothes, and men pressed every kind of bucket into service for carrying water.

On October 8, Edward R. Wren, a heroic leader of the mortar section of the 42nd Division's 167th Infantry in the July battle of Croix Rouge Farm and the recipient of a battlefield commission, wrote his father, "We have few chances to write or do anything else except move and fight and we are still in the advanced zone waiting, listening to the big guns roar. Expect to move up any minute." After writing about men who had been wounded and hospitalized, he concludes, "I hear that we will be able to continue to push the Germans and make them quit entirely."[560]

Maj. Gen. Bullard, who visited the front for a look at the German defenses at the Côte de Châtillon, described the danger facing the 42nd Division in the Argonne: "The way out is forward...through...wire tangled devilishly in forests...pillboxes in succession, one covering another…no 'fox hole' cover for gunners here, but concrete masonry, bits of trenches, more wire, defense in depth."[561]

Putting the Rainbow Division into this battle was part of Pershing's decision to use only experienced fighters in the Argonne. The green ones had mostly failed him. The AEF had forty-two divisions then, with twenty-nine in the line. The best were the 1st, 2nd, 42nd and 89th, and along with the 26th Division, several of those—the 1st, 2nd, and 42nd—were among the "winter divisions," those that would be in France the longest with Pershing.[562] He knew them well and compared all divisions coming into the war with them. After wearing out and using up the 1st Division he replaced it with the 42nd, the best National Guard Division.

Like all other divisions in the Argonne, the Rainbow's move to the front began as a struggle with bad roads and traffic jams. Every village was a total ruin as the regiments halted behind the main battle lines. One historian described how "Craters fifteen feet deep and as wide across pockmarked all sides of the roads. The woods, which had once been thick with stately trees and luxuriant undergrowth, were now a graveyard of mud, broken limbs, and splintered stumps."[563]

Despite the landscape, some things did boost the men's spirits temporarily. Rainbow soldiers in that rear area saw 1st Division soldiers bringing out German prisoners, and their morale was boosted even more when the 42nd Division's 167th and 168th Infantry bands played concerts for everyone. Chaplains led some men in prayer. Camping in pup tents and resting was, relatively speaking, not much of a hardship, but the men still knew that combat was ahead, and that tainted everything.[564]

The 42nd Division established its Post of Command at Cierges-sous-Mountfaucon, with artillery and supply trains of wagons and mules nearby. The stage was set for another Allied push, the third of the Argonne Campaign. The first phase, an offensive led by the 35th Division on September 26, had been disastrous and the next one, led by the 1st Division on September 30, also failed to achieve its objectives. The 42nd Division carried knowledge of those failures, along with the hopes of the entire AEF.

The 42nd Division prepares to relieve the 1st Division

The 165th Infantry

The 42nd Division's 165th Infantry Regiment from New York spent a week in the mud near Exermont while on the way to the front. The highlight of its stay was bread, hot cocoa, and beef served by a nice fat YMCA man in blue overalls and a sombrero. [565]

The regiment, which then consisted of fifty-three officers and nearly 3,000 men, tramped five miles on October 10. [566] There were no trails between the shot-up trees, and every move was with the same old jumble of troops, camions, and wagon trains pulled by mules on slippery roads. [567] It passed the rear of the 1st Division, then went through some 3rd Division supply lines and all of the 32nd Division's supply lines. It ended up in dark woods littered with German and American bodies, grim proof of the 35th Division's trip through the Exermont Ravine before its fighting there ended in failure. [568]

Col. Robert R. McCormick, formerly in the 1st Division, commanding the 122nd Field Artillery of the 33rd Division, with his cousin Captain Joseph Patterson of the 149th Field Artillery of the 42nd Division during the Meuse-Argonne campaign.

The 166th Infantry

At 0430 on October 6 the last mules and wagons of the 42nd Division's 166th Ohio Infantry pulled into the Bois de Montfaucon, the most desolate and depressing area they had ever seen. Rain fell constantly. Every inch of the ground had been torn by shellfire from 1914 and more recent battles. Pup tents and leftover German elephant iron shelters offered the only shelter from cold and rain. Every soldier had only one blanket, and they were all inevitably wet. Despite the fall chill, men wore summer uniforms and underwear issued in August. The regiment's history, written by R.M. Cheseldine, a participant, says "morale was almost gone. Had the Germans known just how low the men were in mind and body, they might have taken courage."[569]

The soldiers' mood further plummeted by watching ambulances with wounded 1st Division men on the way to the rear and hearing the swish of heavy American artillery rounds going overhead. The Ohioans stayed in the mud for a week. The weary men finally moved out of that soggy place to relieve 1st Division units on October 11. A visual recon of the new position took place that morning, and the relief was made on the night of October 11-12.[570] The prospect of imminent battle seemed to raise the dejected spirits of the men of the 166th. [571]

The 167th Infantry

The 42nd Division's 167th Infantry, which hailed from Alabama, started its move to the battlefield area on the afternoon of October 4. The men hiked from Bulainville to Parois, twelve miles west of Verdun, where they spent a frosty night on a hillside. Kitchen trucks brought coffee and a hot breakfast on October 5 before the unit marched through Avocourt, then proceeded west on a line parallel with the front toward the Argonne Forest. Out of caution the regiment took up the combat approach-march formation, with five-yard intervals between men. The men camped in a small wood about two miles east of Exermont.

On October 11, the 167th Infantry marched to the vicinity of Exermont for a visual recon of its assigned sector.[572] Two officers and two noncommissioned officers from each rifle company and people from Machine Gun Company met on the forward slope of Hill 263 for their first look at their primary objective, the Côte de Châtillon.[573]

The 168th Infantry

The 42nd Division's 168th Infantry, an Iowa regiment, began its final move to the front on October 3. The men made long hikes on October 4 and 5 through villages filled with men from other divisions. The Iowans considered it a sure sign that combat was coming when rubber-tired trucks driven by members of the French Army picked them up on the night of October 6, forming a mile-long convoy that set out for Montfaucon.

After an eight-hour drive they dismounted and hiked in the dark before camping in the open among the ruins of Apremont, a place of barbed wire, debris, and caved-in cellars left by the Germans. Nearby forests held skeletons of French soldiers left unburied from battles in 1914. A shack near Company A held the whitened bones of some, along with rotted leather equipment. The Iowans waited in this grim spot, among the debris and shell holes, for five days. Rumors circulated, mostly about the mighty battle that had been underway since September 26. Splintered trees were everywhere, and it was hard to find a place to pitch a tent. The nights were frosty and windy, chilling to the bone.[574]

Still, officials made some attempts to promote leisure activities. The regimental band played on Sunday, October 6, and divine services, the last for some men, were held. After dusk on October 10 the 168th left the mucky shell holes of the Bois de Montfaucon and headed toward the front. They stopped after midnight in formation at the cross roads at Eclisfontaine. A few shells fell south of them, but none came close until the road was blocked by a section of motorized heavy guns. While standing in formation the Iowans were hit with a burst of three shells over the column. There was no warning sound, just exploding shells. A and B Companies suffered forty-seven wounded and six killed, more than the regiment had lost in the entire St. Mihiel operation. Although panic was averted, confusion still existed, as almost always happens in such a crisis. Some companies were split up and not reorganized until daylight.[575]

The march to the front on the next night, October 11-12, took ten hours to go six miles. The men of the 168th put on gas masks near the

Exmorieux Farm. On that wet, cold, and miserable night, the German artillery fired gas shells into low places throughout the area. The gas casualties and the combat approach-march formation made for a long, slow column. When it finally stopped, soldiers scattered through the brush, pitched tents in the dark, and slept briefly, not knowing that they would return to the area a week later with far fewer men, due to casualties.[576]

Most of the 168th's 1st Battalion went into position at the foot of Cote 288 near the Bois de Romagne, though the shorthanded Companies A and B were assigned to Cote 263's eastern slope. The 2nd Battalion crowded in there with the 167th's 2nd Battalion, which was temporarily on the southern slope. The 168th's 3rd Battalion remained in the rear near Exermont, where Col. Matthew A. Tinley established regimental headquarters.[577]

The very close German front line made for a restless night. In the middle of it a battery of US artillery fired short rounds into the position. These short rounds repeated at 0830, but there were no casualties. The 168th made contact on October 12 with Maj. Ravee Norris of the 167th's 3rd Battalion, which was on the 168th's left. (An element of the 32nd Division was on the 168th's right.) Chaplains from the Iowa regiment supervised the burial of over a hundred 1st Division soldiers left on the battlefield. [578]

Days Seventeen and Eighteen: Saturday and Sunday, October 12-13, 1918

The Rainbow Division Artillery comes up

The Rainbow Artillery Brigade had been in combat or on the move in support of the 32nd Division since September 1. It was relieved from that duty at midnight on October 11 and handed back to the 42nd. Eskil Bjork, a discouraged and worn out Rainbow artilleryman, wrote about the move to the front, "we passed through Avoncourt which had been in No-Man's-Land for three years. It was in complete ruins, not one stone left on top of another where evidence showed that there had been houses." When the unit made camp, Bjork described how "what had once been a forest was only a mass of splintered tree trunks and stumps; shell holes were so numerous they overlapped."[579]

Despite such exhaustion, the artillery took some comfort in being back with its division. The Rainbow always attacked with its regiments side by side, making the artillery's job a lot simpler than when there were multiple attacks over multiple fronts. [580] Bjork wrote about supporting other divisions in active combat before returning to his unit in its new position: "If anything we were too exhausted to be prepared for the presence of death. Rather, we felt it offered a way out of this continued misery of going on and on when every thought seemed to demand a continuation of this hell which we call war. We were reaching the breaking point, mentally and physically...at best it was possible to get but two hours of sleep out of 24."[581]

On the afternoon of October 12, the guns were moving through heavy traffic all night on their way to rejoin the division. Artillery recon teams were picking out battery positions and writing orders for them to move. It was after dark before they finished, though they were to commence firing that night. Bjork recalled that the following morning, "the new position came under the searching fire of the Germans forcing the cannoneers to seek the shelter of the flop trenches. Enemy aviators flew low and raked the fields with their machine guns."[582]

The 1st Army pauses

The entire 1st Army in the Argonne paused for two days, October 12 and 13, to prepare for the general attack scheduled for October 14. That left time for the 1st Division to hand the point of V Corps to the 42nd Division. Other than sporadic German artillery fire, the battlefield was quiet.[583]

Despite being side by side, there was little coordination between the Rainbow and the 32nd Divisions, as their orders required separate and independent operations. The 42nd would attack Cote 260 while the 32nd Division aimed at the Côte Dame Marie, and the divisions had different routes to their objectives.[584]

When the 42nd reached the 1st Division after dark on October 11, the Rainbow was unable to straighten its line. The 166th and 165th Infantry Regiments were even with each other and even with the 82nd Division lines on their left, but on the right flank the 167th extended north of the division line by about five hundred yards. To the 167th's rear and slightly to its right stood the 168th Infantry. The four Rainbow infantry regiments were dug in side by side, but the battlefield configuration forced them to be echeloned in irregular steps, causing a staggered front.[585]

On October 13 German artillery fire on the 166th's front supported a weak infantry attack that the Americans easily turned back by mid-afternoon. An unnerving friendly fire episode took place with the 167th's Company K that day, when short rounds killed two men and wounded others.[586] That incident was reported through channels, and a later report of investigation dated October 17, 1918 said, "in every case they have been checked and found to be without foundation."[587]

Preparing for the attack

On the night of October 13, the 166 Infantry Regiment received orders to join in the division-wide attack the following morning.588 All four regiments of the Rainbow were to attack abreast on October 14 at 0830. The two brigades containing the regiments were to draw even during the battle, then go forward abreast of each other. Jump-offs were by the watch. The brigades were to start at the same time and draw even with each other within three hours.589 In addition to the official attack order, at five o'clock Pershing, who wanted more from his soldiers, put out "an order … to the entire 1st Army … the Army must be more aggressive."590

As Pershing exhorted soldiers, a wide, troublesome gap opened between the 167th Alabamians and the 168th Iowans. About seven hundred yards wide, the gap emerged as the result of the 32nd Division on the Rainbow Division's right: "During night of October 13 the 32nd withdrew three hundred meters to permit their artillery to shell a hill in front of them. That flank was for some time entirely open."591 Major Ross of the 168th's 3rd Battalion was ordered to move that regiment's line to the right; he did so without notifying the 167th Alabama on its left. This left room for the Germans to filter in between the Iowans and Alabamians. They put rifle fire into the flanks of both regiments that were scheduled to attack the next day under separate orders.592

Meanwhile, artillery was preparing for the big new attack. An enlisted man with the 150th Field Artillery said, "I suppose we will fire tonight as I was talking to an Alabama infantry replacement…who said they were going over the top in the morning at 0800." He also spoke of buying two bottles of champagne at a village on the way up, saying, "the weather is getting cold and we needed it…the cooties are getting fierce." He had worn the same summer underwear for more than a month and was without a bath the whole time.593

Like other doughboys, the artillerymen lived under primitive conditions. A soldier in the 149th Artillery observed, "It is most difficult to get rations up to such a place and we subsist on stuff called 'camouflage' because it looks and tastes worse than our camouflage nets would have tasted had we put them in a pot of water and boiled them. It is a combination of solidified vegetables that some 'sharpshooter' back in the States had sold the government and probably made millions on it. It comes in five-gallon containers. It keeps one's bowels in a constant state of uproar and dysentery rages rampant in the outfit."594

Still, that night, the artillerymen had something to occupy their thoughts, as American artillery fire began at dark.[595]

CHAPTER 6

The 42nd Division attacks the Côte de Châtillon

The 83rd Infantry Brigade prepares for its attack

Brig. Gen. Michael J. Lenihan, commander of the 42nd Division's 83rd Brigade, called a meeting of his 166th and 165th Infantry commanders and an artillery colonel on October 13. In a hut surrounded by dead Germans and American dead from the 35th and 1st Divisions, they discussed an annex to the original AEF artillery order calling for even fire across the division front. The annex required all possible assistance to the Rainbow Division's 84th Brigade; accordingly, the 83rd would move ahead of the 84th during the imminent battle.[596] The 167th Infantry must advance to the north and cut off German fire being poured into the right flank of the attacking 165th. This problem and others were addressed by changes in the artillery plan.[597]

Its final version called for uniform distribution of fire across the whole front, which meant no regiment or part of the front would be favored by receiving more than an even share of fire support from artillery. That contrasted with General Summerall's usual practice of concentrating fire in that part of the infantry attack that most needed it.[598] During an 83rd Brigade meeting, attendees considered requesting more artillery ammunition, but "the conference broke up without any decisions announced."[599]

Day Nineteen: Monday, October 14, 1918

The 165th (New York) Infantry Regiment begins its attack on the Côte de Châtillon

As V Corps commander, Summerall showed confidence in the 83rd Brigade by choosing it, rather than the 84th Brigade, to make the first assault on the Côte de Châtillon. The 165th Infantry's commander assigned leadership of its attack to Lt. Col. William J. Donovan, the thirty-five-year-old commander of the 3rd "Shamrock" Battalion, who would lead the attack on the ground as de-facto regiment commander. Col. Harry Mitchell, the de-jure commander of the regiment, established headquarters at Exermont in the rear.

Donovan's robust reputation as a combat leader likely contributed to Summerall's decision. Donovan's nickname, "Wild Bill," came from his days as a football player at Columbia University, but he had a distinguished military career. In the attack, Donovan would wear his medals and campaign ribbons, including a US Distinguished Service Cross and a French Croix de Guerre, to inspire a visible sign of authority.

The plan allowed the 165th New Yorkers three hours, beginning at 0830, to attack from the southwest and draw even with the 167th Alabamians on their right. The 165th and 167th Infantry Regiments would then attack side by side, with the 167th cutting off German fire into the 165th's right flank.

American artillery began shelling the German Côte de Châtillon at 0500, and the battle opened at 0830 with Americans attacking the Côte de Châtillon from the southwest, aimed at its right and front. The 165th New Yorkers attacked in clear weather, but they were shorthanded, with lieutenants commanding half of the companies.

German airplanes maintained air superiority while spotting for artillery and machine gunners shooting from Cote 288.[600] Early in the battle, combatants helped evacuate the wounded. There was no tank support.[601]

The New Yorkers were in touch with the Alabamians on their right flank in the beginning, but contact was lost and not regained during the battle. The Alabamians were unable to advance and cut off German fire from the Côte de Châtillon into the 165th.[602] Donovan believed the three hours given him to take the hill were not enough to accomplish the mission.

The New York regiment's 3rd Battalion, on the point and coming from the southwest, reached its first objective after little German resistance and even took some prisoners. The 165th's attacking 2nd

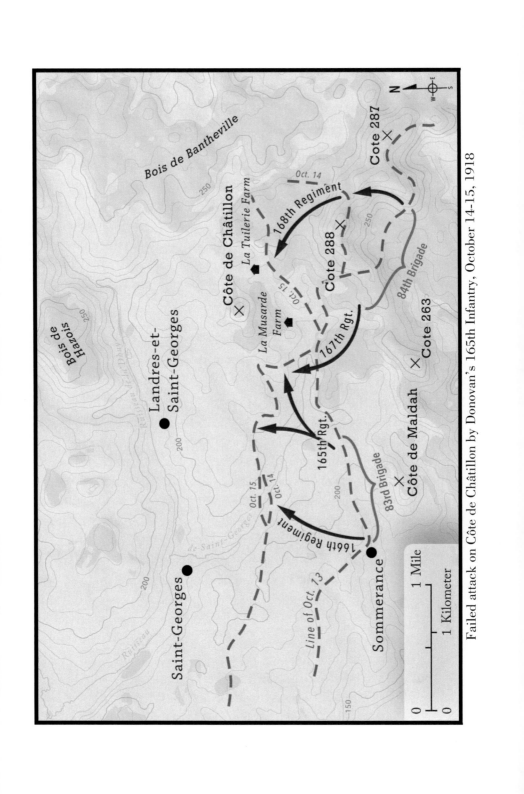

Failed attack on Côte de Châtillon by Donovan's 165th Infantry, October 14-15, 1918

and 3rd Battalions, both commanded by Donovan, reached the second objective, a ridge directly in front of the German wire on the American approach to Landres-et-Saint-Georges. By then the 165th Infantry attack had covered about two miles from jump-off, and a space of only about four hundred yards stood between the New Yorkers and the German wire.[603]

Despite its successful advance, "the 83rd Brigade was in a precarious position."[604] The Germans occupied good defensive positions protected by twenty-foot-wide belts of new barbed wire, three rows of elaborate trenches, and dozens of machine gun positions. Behind those barriers stood two more defensive lines with low wire and shallow trenches. Germans on Cote 260, the Côte de Châtillon, dominated the countryside, an open plain to its right and much of its front to the south.

Donovan conducted the battle from a shell hole near the top of the rise in front of the German barbed wire.[605] The New Yorkers made slow, infiltration-type moves, but few men could move at a time, and any movement was dangerous. Many New Yorkers were killed after reaching the wire, and evacuating casualties proved quite challenging. Some bodies would still remain there weeks later, during the clean-up attack on November 1.[606]

The 165th's Company I took shelter in the sunken Landres-et-Saint-Georges Road and was told to wait until the units on its left and right drew even. Company K was then forced to take shelter with them. The Germans nearly destroyed the 165th's 1st and 3rd Battalions with mortar, rifle, and machine gun fire. A Machine Gun platoon from the 165th lost half its men and two guns there.[607]

The attack, renewed at 1130, failed again. One participant wrote, "The advance did not go well…we fought our way to within 500 meters of the line."[608] Another recalled, "The fighting reached its highest possible point about eleven o'clock that morning and hung at this point all day."[609]

The 165th's position was further compromised by the 167th's failure to advance as planned and cover the 165th's right flank. Because the 167th lagged behind, Germans on the Côte de Châtillon continued firing into the right flank of the attacking New Yorkers.

Royal Little, a Harvard dropout commanding the 167th's Company K on the 165th's right flank said, "About noon on October 14, after visiting all my platoons, I realized what a serious position we were in as K Company's failure to advance was really responsible for all of the adjoining units as well."[610]

Donovan recalled, "It did not look as if that regiment [the 167th] despite its wonderful fighting qualities, could get the Côte de Châtillon before we would find ourselves out in the open catching fire from our right flank."[611] Donovan issued instructions for another attack, commanded by Company C's Capt. Henry Bootz, at 2000 with Companies C and A on line, supported by Companies B and D. Bootz recalled that the attack launched on time, and "the Germans remained silent until the front wave reached the first line of the barbed wire when a terrific machine gun and artillery fire was suddenly let loose by the enemy and German flares transformed night into day. The infantry was unable to penetrate the barbed wire."[612] After the advance was checked, the attacking force retired to the sunken road.

The Rainbow Division 75mms fired 23,000 rounds during the day.[613] American artillery shelled the German Côte de Châtillon for hours, from 0500 to 1700, then resuming around 2000 for the evening attack. Estimates suggest that over 2,723 rounds were fired at the Germans that day.

The Americans suffered heavy casualties during the day's attacks. Engineers and artillery were unable to knock out the German barbed wire, and every soldier reaching it was shot.[614]

Company D's Lt. Dalton Hayes, grandson of Pres. Rutherford B. Hayes, was wounded during the assault. After graduating from the Princeton Officer Training Corps, he had joined the regiment at Camp Mills and was in all its combat operations until wounded. He described the battle in a letter to his mother:

> We were 'moppers up'...immediately behind the first wave...by the way, this was my third time...and at 8:30 all hell came loose from its foundations...I remained unhurt for three hours and by eleven o'clock we'd pushed 'em over two kilometers when suddenly I saw a Jerry[615] about

two hundred yards away aiming a rifle in my direction...Here's where I make my score three instead of two
and I jerked my rifle up...That's the last I remember...Someone got the Boche sniper and the Lord deliver
[sic] me from another ride in a Ford ambulance.[616]

Many men demonstrated courage throughout the battle. James E. Winestock, a private in Company M, 165th Infantry Regiment, showed disregard for personal safety by repeatedly carrying messages from his company commander to the platoon commanders through an area swept by heavy artillery, machine gun fire, and rifle fire. He found eleven men without a leader and took them into the fight.[617] An equally heroic event took place when machine gun fire interrupted the advancing platoon of PFC Robert Riggsby, who was also in Company M. Riggsby went forward alone, killing one, capturing five enemy soldiers, and silencing two machine guns.[618] Capt. Michael J. Walsh, after being wounded, stayed with his company until being killed while trying to dislodge a sniper.[619] Cpl. James O'Connor of the 165th's Company I, the only member of his squad who had not been killed or wounded, killed three Germans and silenced their machine gun by himself before transporting "three of his comrades from their exposed positions to safety."[620] Sgt. Michael A. Donaldson, Company I, under direct observation by the Germans, advanced to the crest of the hill and rescued a soldier. He repeated that act five more times while under fire, for which he received the Medal of Honor.[621]

A high level of fighting quality was evident throughout the attack. Second Lt. Charles A. Huelser, Machine Gun Company, "coolly placed his guns where they could best fire on the advancing enemy" despite his own exposed position.[622] Individual fighting skills and courage were also evident everywhere among the couriers. Pvt. William P. White, Company D, "time and again traversed three kilometers to the front lines with messages," successfully doing that dangerous work where others had failed.[623]

Still, despite the heroics of its men, the 165th concluded the day without reaching its goal, and the Côte de Châtillon remained in German hands.

The 166th Infantry Regiment attacks at the same time as the 165th

One purpose of the October 14 attacks was to even up the 166th (Ohio) Infantry with the 165th, so the 166th was to hold its relative position on the division line north of the destroyed village of Sommerance. The 82nd Division's 325th Infantry, which occupied Sommerance, was in line on the 166th's left. The 165th New York Infantry was on the right on the same line.[624]

The 82nd Division and the 166th jumped off at the same time, approximately 0730. Sixteen tanks were scheduled to attack with the 83rd Brigade, but they did not show up. The 166th reached the woods about seven hundred yards north of Sommerance after following a rolling artillery barrage for fifteen minutes. Company H's Sgt. Irvin H. Dresbach, while severely gassed, commanded both an advance patrol and his platoon when their officers were wounded, causing the enemy facing him to surrender.[625]

At 0740 Companies L and M attacked as assault companies with Companies I and K in support. At 0845 an enemy field piece was seen being dragged from a ridge to the north towards the 166th position. The 82nd Division on the left forced the Germans to pull back.[626] At 0930 a report received from 83rd Brigade headquarters at 0939 advised that the neighboring 165th Infantry on the right was advancing on the Germans and had reached its second objective.[627]

At 0935 the 166th's Company L was held up by machine gun fire at enemy lines 150 yards south of the German trench system. Company M of the 166th reported hard fighting in the woods and the loss of twenty men, with enemy still in front of the regiment. Sgt. Roy Holcomb spent the day with his company, despite being severely gassed.[628] Meanwhile, the 165th Infantry on the 166th's right requested zone artillery fire on its front line to be extended over the brigade front to include the 166th Infantry front. Artillery was ordered to provide sweeping fire to commence at 1015 for battalion commanders to adjust lines.[629]

At 1040 an enemy airplane fired on the 166th's front lines and dropped signals to German artillery. The 166th's infantry patrols went forward to enemy wire south of Saint-Georges but could not hold the position.[630]

The 165th Infantry was to the right and slightly to the rear of the 166th at 1130. Four flights of enemy planes were observed around noon, and one enemy balloon was shot down near Buzancy. No American planes appeared, and the German aircraft operated without interference from Allied air service. The 166th met stubborn resistance at 1255, and nine enemy airplanes fired into them near Sommerance.[631] Indirect fire from German machine guns came from a considerable distance behind the German front lines.[632]

At 1230 the division commander was reportedly anxious for the 166th to get to the heights beyond Landres-et-Saint-Georges. Despite attempts to advance, forward progress stopped at 1530. In late afternoon, the 166th's Company I received a new commander and orders to replace Company L on the front line. The replacement took place at dusk during a German bombardment of gas and high-explosive shells.[633]

At 1440 an American barrage was laid down on German trenches between Saint-Georges and Landres-et-Saint-Georges with maximum fire of one hundred rounds per piece per hour. Fire was then lifted to the stream north of the trenches at the same rate while forward patrols were withdrawn.[634]

At 1835 the nearest infantry of the 165th New Yorkers were seen scattering on the 166th's right, with officers trying to round their soldiers up.[635] After his platoon commander was killed, Sgt. Michael F. Fitzpatrick took command. Although he incurred a wound near the start of the engagement and endured constant exposure to gas and fire, he stayed in command until his platoon's relief "late that night, when he was evacuated" for treatment.[636]

A line was organized for the 166th that night, linking it with the 165th on the right and the 82nd Division on the left. Still, a gap of about seven hundred yards existed between the 166th and 165th Regiments.[637]

The 166th made no attack, but its men did try to infiltrate by stealth.[638] An order came at 1930 for the 166th to send patrols out that night. The Ohioans penetrated until meeting resistance. At 2250 an order from 83rd Brigade required the 166th's 3rd Battalion to relieve the 2nd Battalion during the night.

The 166th's attack was not progressing, and the regiment

suffered 267 casualties on October 14.[639] Summerall, displeased at the results of the attack, said, "The left brigade (the 83rd) gained little ground and was stopped before Landres-et-Saint-Georges even though this attack was supported by the artillery of the First, Forty-second and Thirty-second Divisions."[640]

The division was ordered to attack again on the next day, October 15, and to continue until the Côte de Châtillon was taken. No divisions on the right or left would advance in the meantime.[641]

Day Twenty: Tuesday, October 15, 1918

The 165th (New York) Infantry Regiment fails in its attack

On the morning of October 15, the 165th's 1st Battalion, with Maj. John Kelly commanding, renewed the New Yorkers' attack. They were scheduled to link up with tanks, which did not arrive.

Casualties were heavy from the beginning, especially among messengers. Cpl. Matthew George Rice of Company A carried a message under fire, while wounded, from the regimental commander to the assault battalion and returned with another message.[642] Pvt. John Hammond, having seen four messengers killed while trying "to reach headquarters with an important position sketch," carried the message successfully.[643] Though he was wounded on the journey, Cpl. Thomas O'Kelly carried a message to regimental headquarters, despite seeing all the battalion runners before him killed or wounded on the same mission.[644] Pvt. Matthew Joseph Kane repeatedly volunteered to be a messenger after others became casualties.[645] Pvt. Frederick P. Craven also volunteered for messenger duty when all other messengers had been killed or wounded; he made the trip and returned successfully.[646]

Some enlisted leaders took the places of lost officers. Sgt. Spiros Thomas, born in Greece, of Company B, after losing all his officers and a 1st Sergeant, assumed command of his shorthanded unit and led it throughout the day.[647]

Capt. Oscar L. Buck, although wounded, led his company successfully and refused evacuation, continuing "to direct his men under terrific artillery and machine gun fire."[648] While above the enemy's wire and under intense fire, Sgt. Thomas F. Fitzsimmons of Headquarters Company disrupted a threatened counterattack, with support from mortars.[649]

Even Donovan was hit by a sniper.[650] Unable to walk or lead the fight, he ordered Kelly's 1st Battalion, his replacement for the 3rd Battalion Shamrocks, to turn back, thereby ending the 165th's attack. However, Kelly would not withdraw until Donovan gave the order in writing.[651]

About noon the advance was held up due to the fire from the Côte de Châtillon. Company C's 1st Sgt. Thomas P. O'Hagan, born in Ireland, was killed rescuing a soldier while under direct machine gun fire. On the previous day, he had conducted a raid and returned to his lines, immediately going back amid more exposure to fire to rescue a soldier a hundred yards from enemy wire.[652]

Incoming fire on its right flank (from the Côte de Châtillon) was "the primary cause for the failure of the 83rd Brigade to break through and for the delay in capturing the Côte de Châtillon."[653] According to Duffy, "Conditions on the right made it impossible to reach the wire with strength enough to penetrate."[654]

Though the 165th needed the planned support from the 167th, the Alabamians were unable to advance sufficiently due to their own challenging circumstances. Men struggled to evacuate their casualties under heavy German fire, though Company G's Cpl. Moses S. Baldwin "repeatedly went over shell-swept areas under heavy machine-gun fire to give first-aid treatment to the wounded and carry them to shelter."[655] Company H's Sgt. Lee Wadsworth distinguished himself by remaining with his unit despite being wounded. In defiance of his severe wounds, Wadsworth aided his platoon in preparing for an imminent counterattack, "thereby setting to his men an inspiring example of utter disregard for danger and heroism in the face of the enemy."[656]

Meanwhile, the 165th continued fighting valiantly. Before the end of the attack, Cpl. Charles Cain risked fire to acquire ammunition for his unit, which had used its entire supply. He made repeated trips to remove ammunition from the dead.[657] Sgt. Edward P. Clowe, Company C, led his section under heavy machine gun fire. Having been stopped, he maintained the position four hours until ordered to withdraw, at which time he helped evacuate wounded men, then served as rear guard with several others. He "continued to resist superior numbers of enemy until he fell mortally wounded" behind enemy lines.[658] With another soldier, Pvt. Archibald Reilly, Company C, rescued a wounded man fifty yards beyond his lines, risking fire to transport the man to safety.[659] Sgt. John Patrick Furey, Company H, while wounded and under fire, went to the aid of a soldier wounded in both legs. He got the man to the aid station, returned to the battle, and incurred another wound.[660]

The promised orders to withdraw came at 1530. At about four o'clock five German planes circled and bombed the remains of the 3rd Battalion. That was followed by German 155 artillery fire. What was left of the battalion was sent to the Côte de Maldah after dark.[661] With so many casualties taken, wounded had to be evacuated under highly dangerous conditions. Cpl. Joseph W. Burns and another soldier rescued a wounded man beyond the lines.[662] Donovan remained in position for five hours before being evacuated.

During the battle, five of the regiment's fifty-three officers were killed, and twenty were wounded.[663] Wounded were evacuated and withdrawal completed at 1800.[664]

The 166th (Ohio) Infantry Regiment fails in its attack

Throughout October 15, the 166th Infantry, attacking in the direction of Landres-et-Saint-Georges, also struggled to meet its objective. At 0925 the 166th's Company M reported hard fighting with the Germans still in the woods. Meanwhile, the 82nd Division advance on the left of the 166th was held up.[665] Furthermore, a tank commander reported that Germans on the right of the 165th Infantry were getting the better of the Americans.[666]

Things continued dismally for the 166th. At 1324 that afternoon its Company M reported that its four attempts to advance were unsuccessful; it accumulated sixty casualties that afternoon. At 2200 the battalion adjutant reported that fifty men would be ordered from the 117th Engineers as carrying parties for Bangalore Torpedoes.

Messengers demonstrated particular valor for the cause that day. Pvt. Adam H. Pyles repeatedly carried messages over territory covered by snipers, machine guns, and artillery until, caught in the heavy fire, he was killed.[667] Pvt. George Brenstuhl was one of only two men running messages for his company that day. When he witnessed the other messenger's death, Brenstuhl risked fire to retrieve the dead soldier's message and complete his mission.[668]

H. H. Grave, who was evacuated about 1700 that afternoon, wrote, "Several times during the day slight advances were made by the 3rd Battalion of the 166th but no material gain was made...airplanes on our side were nonexistent while German planes were plentiful and directed intense fire on us practically all-day long."[669]

In the face of such an enemy presence, all the 166th's attacks on October 15 were unsuccessful. The regiment's casualties for the day were 18 killed, 132 wounded, and 28 missing.[670]

The 168th Iowa Infantry attacks Hill 288

Artillery barrages went out all night on October 14 in preparation for the 168th (Iowa) regiment to jump off at 0530 on October 15.[671] The regiment had reached the crest of Cote 288 and cleared much of the forward slope attack the day before, and the same soldiers would set out again to clear all of Cote 288 and the east and west slopes of Cote 242 to the north.

Before the battle opened as planned, 3rd Battalion brought up hot food, while whole platoons from some companies helped as stretcher bearers and with ammunition details, dangerous work conducted under the watchful eyes of enemy snipers. Trees held German wire obstructions, and enemy gas and friendly short rounds came in, as the line for the night ran three hundred yards south of the Tuilerie Farm, around the forward slope of Cote 242, and southwest along the clearing in front of the Musarde Farm. Near a hedge just over the ridge beyond the farm, the ground dipped and rose again, marking an area of small plots of farmland divided by hedgerows. The open land extended to the border of the woods covering the Côte de Châtillon's southern slope, then extended to the right to within a hundred yards of the Tuilerie Farm. The 168th Infantry tried to pass through the heavily defended the Tuilerie Farm three different times before it finally "advanced the center of the V Corps one step further towards its objective," and came face-to-face with the Germans on the Côte de Châtillon's southeastern slope.[672]

In the attack on October 15, Companies B and D advanced toward the left of Cote 242, and Company A went around the right. The mortar platoon accompanied them. They encircled the hill, took it, and cleared the last formidable obstacle to taking all of the Côte de Châtillon.[673]

Lieutenant Breslin led a platoon of Iowans for more than half a mile into the Tuilerie Farm, taking out two machine guns. The success was costly. Only twelve men remained in the platoon when Lt. Howard G. Smith continued its fight with the help of a sergeant, two corporals, and others. Before noon they took sixty Germans prisoner.[674]

Machine gun fire from the Côte de Châtillon forced Company A back to the edge of the Bois de Romagne, where it went into a line with the battalion's other companies. There was a heavy bombardment for an hour and a half. The 151st Field Artillery fired about a thousand rounds in support of the 168th as it fought toward Cote 260 that afternoon. Losses were high.[675] Lt. William R. Witherell led his company in an attack toward the Côte de Châtillon that took sixty-three prisoners.[676]

The 168's entire 1st Battalion was committed to the fight, though it suffered many casualties and was "reduced to a small band of exhausted men to whom the danger of death was as nothing to the torture of living."[677] The 2nd Battalion's Company F was brought in for support. But all of the line of attack on October 15 was stopped by heavy German machine guns well-placed along the base of the Côte de Châtillon. On the night of October 15, the Iowans lay in flooded and cold foxholes as German flares lighted the battlefield.

Reassessing the 42nd Division's plan

By the end of October 15, the 165th Infantry had made two

unsuccessful assaults on the Côte de Châtillon, and the 166th Infantry tried without success to attack in the direction of Landres-et-Saint-Georges.[678] This ended the 83rd Brigade's part in the fight.

On October 15, General Pershing paid a visit to the headquarters of the 42nd Division.[679] During the dark, rainy night, Summerall visited the Post of Command of the 166th Ohio Infantry and met with its commander, Colonel Hough. He had earlier indicated that Hough might be relieved, but that did not happen.[680] Summerall later described the visit:

> As soon as the lines were stabilized for the day [October 15] I went to see the troops of the Forty-second Division…I found that the division commander [Maj. Gen. Charles T. Menoher] had never left his command post, which was far to the rear and knew almost nothing of the situation at the front. The commander of the left brigade, Brigadier General Michael Lenihan, was confused and completely unstrung. He knew nothing of why the brigade had not advanced and had never left his command post. I…decided to relieve him…On arriving at the command post of the nearest regiment, I found the Colonel starting to Brigade headquarters. He knew nothing of why the regiment had not advanced and had never left his command post…[I] told the division commander what I had seen. I directed him to move his command post forward and to visit his commanders…I found I should have relieved him…I also told him to relieve the brigade commander…Also, I told him to relieve the colonel of the infantry regiment.[681]

By the end of the war, nearly fourteen hundred commanders, ranging in rank from second lieutenant to major general, had been either reassigned or sent back to the United States.[682] Several changes of command were announced by the 83rd Brigade that night. Reilly succeeded Lenihan as commander of the 83rd Brigade, and Lt. Col.

Dravo, the division's machine gun officer, replaced Mitchell as the 165th Infantry's commander. The adjutant and deputy adjutant of the 165th were relieved.

Batteries A, B, C, and F of the 151st Field Artillery suffered casualties on the night of October 15 while German artillery was active.[683] Neither regiment of the 83rd Brigade attacked on October 16.[684]

The battle had gone poorly during the Rainbow's first days at the Côte de Châtillon. In addition to failure to take the objective, it almost ran out of ammunition. One soldier recalled,

> The driver who went on an ammunition detail early that evening did not arrive at the position until just before morning due to the congestion. The crew of the 3rd Section had just fired their last shell when the first caisson came into sight and the other sections were in almost the same fix. Shells were taken off the caissons, 'fuzzed' (fuses set) and shoved into the guns to maintain an uninterrupted fire. One after another caisson was galloped up and discharged its load with two of the drivers assisting in the unloading while the crews served the guns.[685]

The horses were also in terrible condition. It was impossible to get trucks to haul hay, so the horses, starved for want of proper forage, ate carriage wheel spokes, the leather straps of limbers, and tree bark.[686]

As a result of all these factors, the 42nd's early days at the Côte de Châtillon proved bleak and dispiriting.

The 84th Infantry Brigade prepares to attack the Côte de Châtillon

After the 83rd Brigade's failure, some senior officers doubted that MacArthur could take the Côte de Châtillon with his 84th Brigade alone.[687] He shared the sentiment, admitting, "when General Menoher, the Division Commander, asked me whether or not I could take the Côte de Châtillon, I told him as long as we were speaking in strictest confidence that I was not certain."[688]

MacArthur proceeded by asking Colonel Hughes, the 42nd Division's Chief of Staff, for permission to concentrate his attack on the Côte de Châtillon and further requesting that the 151st Minnesota Field Artillery be placed under his command for the coming battle. The requests were granted.

On October 15 Summerall visited MacArthur at la Neuve Forge, a frame house about three miles to the rear of the Côte de Châtillon that served as 84th Brigade headquarters. One version of it said the meeting was brief and to the point, with Summerall saying, "Give me Châtillon, MacArthur, or a list of five thousand casualties." MacArthur replied that if the brigade failed to capture the objective, Summerall could "publish a casualty list of the entire Brigade with the Brigade Commander's name at the top." MacArthur reported that Summerall, visibly moved, left without replying.[689]

Lt. Col. Walter E. Bare, who commanded the 167th, explained the story differently. Bare's version had MacArthur pledging himself and his soldiers in a telephone conference that night with Summerall, Menoher, Winn, Bare, and Col. Tinley. MacArthur was expecting an important telephone call, Bare said, and when it came, "General Summerall was on the line. We could hear his verbal order over the telephone to the effect that the Côte de Châtillon was the key to the whole situation and that he wanted it taken by 6:00 p.m. the next evening."[690]

The plan for the 151st Machine Gun Battalion

As part of the 84th Brigade, the 151st (Georgia) Machine Gun Battalion planned for its upcoming attack on the Côte de Châtillon. MacArthur knew the battalion had taken heavy losses in late July and early August, 1918, when it was "improperly employed" while attacking the heights overlooking the Ourcq River.[691] Though these events transpired before MacArthur, a colonel who served as the 42nd Division Chief of Staff, replaced Brig. Gen. Robert A. Brown as commander of the 84th Brigade, he had learned from the battalion's experience.[692]

The 151st well understood the tactic of using indirect fire over the heads of attacking infantrymen, such as the 1st Division had done previously in the Argonne campaign.[693] The 151st had executed similar tactics on September 23, 1918, in a "come and go" raid following the big attack at St. Mihiel. In that operation, the 151st Machine Gun Battalion supported four infantry platoons from the 167th's Company M, under Capt. Maurice W. Howe. While the infantrymen crept to within three hundred yards of the village, forty-eight of the 151st's machine guns fired over the heads of the infantrymen in the dark at 0430. In that successful attack, each platoon cleaned out a quadrant of the objective and reported back to the raid commander. They killed fifteen and took sixteen prisoners, while losing one killed and four wounded.

From then on, MacArthur had Maj. Cooper D. Winn Jr., who commanded the 151st, report directly to him.[694] This direct report of a battalion commander to a brigade commander departed from common practice, as machine gun battalions typically reported to the infantry battalion or regimental commanders to which they were assigned and who deployed them as they wished. It was further unusual in that Winn, age thirty-eight, was older than MacArthur, who was only thirty-two. Still, the arrangement worked well, and Winn worked with his subordinates to plan upcoming attacks. MacArthur totally backed the plan to attack with indirect fire, which Winn called "a machine gunner's dream."[695] One of the platoon leaders said, "We were of much more benefit to the infantry under this plan than in advancing with them."[696]

On October 12, 1918, the 151st (Georgia) Battalion under Winn had taken up firing positions on the forward slope of Cote 263 in preparation for the October 16, 1918, operation against Cote 260. MacArthur approved the order laying out the tactic. In moving up the battalion passed many unburied German dead, several wounded Germans, and graves of Americans from the 1st Division. They also came under fire from German flat trajectory 77s, machine guns, and artillery controlled by forward observers on 260. There was also incoming German mortar fire from Cote 288. Snipers from the Côte de Châtillon fired at them every time a head was raised, and they were gassed often, making it standard procedure to sleep wearing gas masks. Winn's carefully prepared plan used every gun in the battalion, including any spares and the French-manufactured 64 Hotchkiss machine guns. None had full crews, and all dug in with overhead protection from shrapnel. The guns were put in position through mud and muck with two-wheeled carts pulled by a single mule for which there was little hay and grain. Manpower muscled the guns into place.

During the first two days of attacks on the Côte de Châtillon the machine gun battalion placed barrages on the Tuilerie Farm and Cote 242. Results were limited by dense woods. Gunners had problems seeing the attacking American infantry through the underbrush, and they were often under heavy artillery fire.

Matters were better for the October 14 and October 16 attacks on the Côte de Châtillon, as men had good visibility and an open field of fire on the hill's forward slope. The very precise attack plan for October 16 called for thirty minutes of fire prior to the jump-off of the infantry attack, along with fifteen minutes of fire after the initial assault. Fire would then shift to the hill's reverse slope, with indirect fire on the withdrawing Germans.[697] A group of fir trees stood near the highest point of Cote 260, and its center was the sole reference point from which the machine guns were all sighted. Winn personally checked the laying of every gun.

Almost any target on the hill was within both the gunners' sight and their guns' range. Each gun was assigned a target area fifty meters wide, and each gunner received in writing a specific target with range (elevation) and deflection (horizontal direction and distance). Some were given individual targets, such as trench lines, the hand-operated railroad line near the top of the hill, approaches to concrete bunkers, and other conspicuous points.[698]

The machine gun barrage was more effective than an artillery barrage, which typically used the French 75, a flat trajectory artillery piece that could shoot at only what the gunner saw. In contrast, Winn's machine guns were expected to create such a hail of indirectly fired bullets that German machine gunners on the Côte de Châtillon would be driven to take shelter and stop their outgoing fire.

CHAPTER 7

The 42nd Division captures the Côte de Châtillon

Day Twenty-One: Wednesday, October 16, 1918

The 168th (Iowa) attacks the Côte de Châtillon from the west

The 168th had fought its own hard battle to capture the Tuilerie Farm, and its men spent the early morning of October 16 reorganizing their position. Company D on the left and Company A on the right formed local support, while Company F was placed in the assault line. The attack was ordered for 1000 to coordinate with fire from the 151st Machine Gun Battalion.

Maj. Lloyd D. Ross, commanding the 168th, told the officers of the 1st Battalion, Companies F and H, that the Côte was to be taken that day. Lt. William R. Witherell of the 168th's Company C, wrote, "We were told that if we did not take the Côte in that morning attack that we would reform at 1400 and try again in the afternoon."[699]

For the last of five successive attacks on Cote 260, two companies lined up left to right on October 16, then advanced toward the hedge at 0830. The point of the battalion came out from cover of the woods and started up the meadow in open ranks. The Germans waited until the men came to the swale's ridge before cutting loose with machine guns, direct fire 88s, and rifles. The Iowa skirmish lines continued with bayonets fixed. Companies C and B broke into a run toward the hedge. After about twenty shots the German riflemen ran for the woods.[700]

After a previous withdrawal, the men retook the Tuilerie Farm, along with its entire spur north. Throughout the day, the men would continue to take the farm, then withdraw due to enemy fire. Local strong points were taken on the left and right. The advance continued up the hill, but the Germans put the attackers under heavy fire from the crest. This forced two companies, one of which lost all its officers, to withdraw to the woods on the west of the farm. The Germans followed this up with an attack, but it was stopped by accurate American artillery fire.[701]

Light artillery and four guns from the 168th's Machine Gun Company on Cote 288 put a barrage on the Germans on the Côte de Châtillon for half an hour. At 1030 the attacking Iowans went forward again. They were raked by bullets from the Côte de Châtillon when they hit the open swale that sloped gently uphill from the Musarde Farm to the Tuilerie Farm. All Iowans who advanced beyond the hedge were stopped cold.

Companies H and C rushed forward. There was a break in the action, and the Iowans took advantage of the lull by making a wild attack on the woods at the Côte de Châtillon's base. Eight men were killed and some wounded, but the remainder broke through the woods and took out two machine guns operating against the Tuilerie Farm and Companies H and F. The last of the Stokes Mortar ammunition forced Germans to crowd into a trench leading to a well-constructed concrete dugout.

In the early forenoon the 168th's Company H came from the right of Cote 242 and made it to the woods of the Côte de Châtillon in front of the Tuilerie Farm. The Germans cut loose on it with artillery. The Iowans withdrew a hundred yards to the edge of the Bois de Romagne and dug in at their original position. The 1st Battalion's Company H suffered heavy losses, including the company commander, and was so reduced in size that the remainder of the regiment was put into the battle.[702] Cptn. Glenn C. Haynes, in his capacity as battalion commander, also handled two rifle companies when their commanders were wounded.

Witherell described how in the afternoon when the 167th advanced uphill to Hill 260 "the 168th again attacked, reaching and holding the crest to the right of the hill but was unable to hold it due to enemy crossfire."[703]

Eventually both regiments progressed toward the left of the line. The Tuilerie Farm was taken and passed through as troops headed uphill to the Côte de Châtillon. A German force of four machine guns

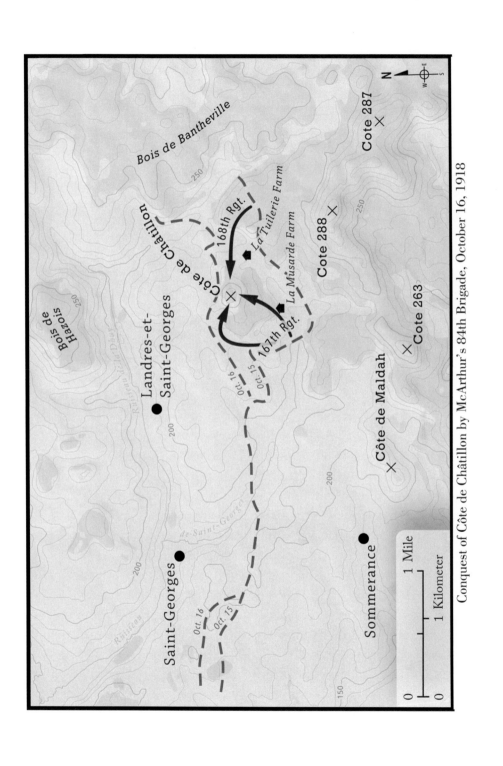

Conquest of Côte de Châtillon by McArthur's 84th Brigade, October 16, 1918

and twenty men was overrun at the edge of the hill. Enemy machine guns hit the assault troops with a hail of fire in the open field between the Musarde Farm and the Tuilerie Farm, but every man in the 168th kept up steady fire.

The Musarde Farm, at the foot of the Côte de Châtillon, November 1918.

The Iowans in the hedge on the left exchanged rifle and machine gun fire with the Germans in the woods to the north. The 168th's entire 1st Battalion was on the front. Ross asked for 2nd Battalion's Company F, which had been in action for three days, and it was sent up. Company D on the battalion's left made contact with the Alabamians during the day but was unable to make a material advance.

At 1530 E and G Companies came into the fight on the extreme right about four hundred yards northeast of the Tuilerie Farm along the narrow-gauge railroad. About that time the 167th advanced and reached the crest of the Côte de Châtillon. The last element of the Iowans reached the crest of the Côte at about 1640, joining the Alabama troops as they reached the summit. The regiments would share equal honors for capturing that vital position.

William Amerine later described how the event transpired: "Only the Alabama companies on the regiment's right were in conjunction with Iowa attackers on the hill. They were Alabama M, one half of F, one half of K and L of the 167th. By moving five hundred yards to the right on the night before, these troops went inside the enemy's wire in the 168th sector. They turned northward until a hedge on the left of the hill was reached just in front of the Côte de Châtillon, where the Alabama attack was launched." [704]

Swedish-born 1st Lt. Oscar B. Nelson had earned everyone's admiration that day by first attacking alone two enemy machine guns, killing two enemy soldiers, and capturing nineteen. Later, he and six other soldiers "advanced 600 yards beyond his own lines through heavy fire from enemy artillery, machine-guns, and rifles, and captured two more machine-guns, killing, capturing, or dispersing their crews." He would finally lead his company on an attack on the Côte de Châtillon, incurring wounds in the process and dying shortly afterwards. [705]

The 168th's 1st Battalion suffered 440 casualties, 70 dead, in five attacks over three days. Other units in the regiment suffered 250 wounded and 17 dead. Still, with the 167th, the regiment had succeeded in achieving what other regiments across several divisions had not been able to accomplish, and the attack was considered the most scientifically fought and most skillfully directed of all the regiment's actions. [706]

The 167th (Alabama) attacks and takes the Côte de Châtillon

At dusk on October 15, Company I's Robert H. Fallaw of Waverly,

The Côte de Châtillon, October 28, 1918.

Alabama, the senior captain of the 3rd Battalion, received orders to attack the Côte de Châtillon, in conjunction with the 168th Infantry on his right, on October 16. His force of about a hundred men came from the four companies of the 167th's 3rd Battalion. Fallaw, a mustang from former enlisted service on the

Mexican Border, was commissioned at Camp Mills as his rifle company from Opelika, Alabama, departed for France. Once there, he became de facto battalion commander, though the title was being handed around. A Company F officer later wrote, "Captain Fallaw organized, directed and carried through to successful completion all of the front-line activities of the 167th on October 16, 1918."[707]

The plan involved careful coordination, because it required the 167th to pass through the 168th's sector through an open space, a passage called a chicane, in the German wire in front of the 167th at the base of the Côte de Châtillon. The chicane was formerly used to allow passage of reliefs and supplies for the Germans occupying it before they were pushed back by the 1st Division, and it was located about five hundred yards to the right of the 167th's position north of the Musarde Farm. Maj. Ravee Norris later described his understanding of the plan: "While the overhead machine gun and the artillery concentration were keeping the Germans down I would send about a hundred men . . . along the hedge which ran from the edge of my wood up to the gap in the wire. From this they could reach a hedge which ran parallel to the southeast face of the Cote de Chatillon [sic] . . . then when the artillery and machine gun fire lifted and the Germans expecting a frontal attack from the west . . . they would be caught in the flank by my hundred men."[708]

The Iowans understood the plan and approved the Alabamians' encroachment into their sector. On the night of October 15, Fallaw and his men moved right about five yards to the open space and crossed through the wire at the chicane. They then turned northeast until stopping at a hedge in front and left of the Côte de Châtillon.

At 0610 on October 16 Fallaw put his men in a skirmish line concealed by the hedge. Norris, who commanded the 3rd Battalion before handing it to Fallaw, kept the attack going forward by maintaining the rear, preventing stragglers and reorganizing casuals. German wire was on the hill's left side, just outside the wood, but it abruptly stopped part of the way up. Fallaw advanced his men to where the wire stopped and set them up to attack beyond it, organizing a "council of war" in which everyone agreed to charge in mass across the open hill to their front, on which there was no German wire.

Everything was in place to take the hill: the 167th was in position on the left, and the 168th had orders to assault the Côte de Châtillon from the right after taking the Tuilerie Farm. Still, the brigade commander could not ensure unbroken communication with his brigade's two front-line battalions, as "the enemy's terrific fire…made it impossible to maintain either Signal Corps installations or runner service." A French liaison officer, Capt. Maurice Drouhin volunteered, at the deadliest risk to himself, "to make his way across a gap between the two battalions in order to carry orders to [their] commanding officers." He was awarded a Distinguished Service Cross for this action.[709]

From the upper slope of Cote 263, Major Winn was set to execute his plan for the 151st Machine Gun Battalion's barrage. At about 1000 all of the machine guns of the 151st opened fire, drawing from a supply of a million rounds that had been brought to the hill under terrible conditions during the previous four days. The machine guns fired steadily for thirty minutes over the heads of the 167th's waiting infantrymen, some of whom said the fire sounded like a million bees overhead. Immediately after the machine gun fire stopped, three whistle blasts signaled the jump-off, and Fallaw and his men rushed forward to the woods on Cote 260's northern edge. Running across the hill, they came under heavy German machine gun fire from the edge of the woods.

Some men demonstrated great valor during the attack. After his platoon commander had been severely wounded and his unit cut to pieces, Sgt. Grady Parrish "quickly reorganized the remainder of the platoon and personally led it in the attack on the Côte de Châtillon. By his daring acts, coolness, and good judgment, he broke up a heavy enemy counterattack on his front."[710] Cpl. Harold Thomson, assisted by several others, "pushed out on the right flank of his company, and, by well directed [sic] fire, gained fire superiority… captured eight of the enemy, including an officer, and drove off a large number of others."[711]

In a particularly inspiring incident, Sgt. Ralph Atkinson of Montgomery's Regimental Mortar Section had a Stokes Mortar and three men, one to observe fire and call corrections to him, and two for helping with ammunition. They were advancing with the assault element when it was stopped by a large force of Germans forming for a counterattack. Holding the mortar tube between his legs while under heavy fire, Atkinson broke up their attack and forced the Germans to retreat.[712] Lt. Harley Banks, who was in the middle of the fight with Company M, wrote: "This particular action was one of the most thrilling of the war to our men."[713] As Atkinson's observer, Cpl. John C. Austin crawled forward fifty yards in the open to select targets and adjust fire. From that position, he also retrieved a wounded comrade and carried him to safety while under machine gun fire.[714]

The soldiers pushed back the Germans developing a second counterattack in an attempt to retake the position. The 5th Field Artillery covered the northern slopes of the hill with well-placed barrages put there by the Artillery Liaison Officer. The German attack broke in confusion.

A second German counterattack at 1500 involved about two hundred Germans reorganized after their retreat through the woods. During that fight an automatic rifleman in Company M, Pvt. Thomas S. Neibaur of Sugar City, Idaho, was shot three times after his loader and scout were killed. He fired fifty rounds into about forty attackers, killing many of them before he was cornered. After being taken prisoner for a short time he recovered a pistol with seven rounds, then killed four Germans and captured eleven, all in full view of his fellow soldiers. A replacement who had fought in every battle since the Champagne, Neibaur became the first Mormon and the second man from the 167th Infantry to receive the Congressional Medal of Honor.[715]

As the 3rd Battalion forces under Fallaw bolted for the summit, elements of the 168th's 1st Battalion retook the open ridge on the right and connected with Alabama troops across the hill to the left. The objective, which had been outlined in a field order, was attained, and the enemy immediately launched a counterattack that was beaten off.[716] The Iowa and Alabama regiments established a line at the top of the hill and put outposts in place.

The two groups drove the Germans over the hill and down the

reverse slope toward Landres-et-Saint-Georges. Any German not killed, wounded, or captured promptly ran north. Norris recalled that Fallaw's men "established a line across the northern slope of the Côte de Châtillon…to our right. This line was continued by the Iowans. The attackers from the 168th began to converge on the hill with the Alabama troops."[717]

Fallaw pressed on to keep the Germans from reorganizing. Norris, who had been hit in the foot by a shell fragment, described it: "Fallaw's attack cleaned up the attack on our side of the hill and then broke out on the left-rear of the Germans. The machine guns opened fire for another fifteen minutes and adjusted fire to the reverse slope, the back side of Cote 260."[718]

Fallaw received a Distinguished Service Cross for gaining the 84th Brigade's final objective "with a minimum loss to his command."[719]

Royal Little, commander of Company K, organized a group of about a hundred men from 2nd Battalion on the left side of the hill. He brought them into the 167th attack in the afternoon to join the 3rd Battalion under Fallaw. Little recalled the attack's significant events:

> Perhaps the most important detail …of that engagement was the counterattack on the Côte de Châtillon at the railroad embankment. I always felt this small local action was of considerable importance in the events of that day and the following days…We took possession of their trenches and barricaded them on the north to prevent a counterattack through the trench. We then extended our point eastward along the northern edge of the Côte until we liaised with the rest of the regiment that had been engaged in a sharp counterattack along the narrow-gauge railroad embankment just south of the crest of Hill 260.[720]

After the Côte de Châtillon was secured by Fallaw's 3rd Battalion, the 2nd Battalion advanced from its support position on Cote 263, taking two companies around the east side of Hill 263 and two companies around the west side, meeting in the Bois de Romagne.

The 151st Minnesota Field Artillery's support was especially effective against a group of about two hundred Germans gathering for a counterattack. A few words were spoken into a field telephone and they were shelled almost immediately by the 151st. Its commander, Col. George Leach, recalled, "The Infantry fought all day for the woods on the cote de Chatillon. [*sic*] We shelled it continually and fired on fleeting targets and at dark our Infantry was in the edge of the woods. A very difficult job with heavy casualties. It must be expressly noted that the Germans here never give up. But die fighting."[721] Later, the 151st's official history described the significance of its contributions, noting, "The artillery support rendered by the 151st in operations against the Côte de Châtillon marks perhaps the highest achievement of the regiment during the war."[722]

Brigadier General MacArthur was not on the Côte de Châtillon when his men took it on October 16, 1918, but the 84th Brigade's victory made his reputation. The brigade's total casualties were smaller than those incurred during the 83rd Brigade's failed attempt to storm the Côte de Châtillon from the left. The 167th Infantry had 81 killed, 36 dead of wounds, and 554 wounded. The 168th Infantry lost 90 killed, 53 dead of wounds, and 566 wounded.[723]

The 167th's 1st Battalion completed the relief of its 2nd Battalion at 0200 on October 17, finally concluding the battle to take the Côte de Châtillon.

Pershing's 1st Army gained a significant objective by taking and holding the Côte de Châtillon on October 16th. Although he had hoped to grab this crucial layer of the German Hindenburg Line weeks earlier when Meuse-Argonne kicked off, Pershing was pleased that the ground was now in American hands, but of course it saddened him that so much blood had been shed by brave doughboys in his 1st, 35th, and 42nd Divisions.

In the overall scheme of the forty-seven day battle, this victory meant that the American doughboys were finally grasping how to outfight the far more experienced German troops. Back in Berlin the beleaguered German government knew this, too, and it was only a matter of time before its troops in the field were soundly defeated. Other losses inflicted by the British and French armies elsewhere on the Western Front promoted talk of an armistice. But that too was a slow process, and the war and tremendous casualties continued for almost another month.

CONCLUSION

General Menoher, the Rainbow Division commander, later sent a telegram to the V Corps Commander General Summerall, saying, "Hills 288, 242 and Côte de Châtillon formed an extraordinary strong bastion in the German line which had resisted repeated attacks. The 84th Brigade was put into the line to capture this position. This was accomplished only after the most desperate fighting through wire and trenches against a resolute and determined defense involving frequent and bitter counterattacks. The enemy's machine guns raked our lines from flank and rear and the situation became most critical...on a field where courage was the rule."[724]

General Pershing would write after the Côte de Châtillon was cleared, "The main objective of our initial attack on September 26 had now been reached."[725] Still, though, some skirmishes continued. The Alabama regiment had 117 men killed and 566 wounded after the Côte de Châtillon fell and while peace was being negotiated. Its sister regiment in the 84th Brigade, the 168th Infantry, suffered similarly high losses in the final days of combat, as its head count was fewer by 1,150 men and 25 officers than it had been at the beginning of the battles six days earlier.[726]

The 42nd Division ultimately received, "at home and abroad about 20,000 replacements for its authorized strength of 28,000 men."[727] It participated in five of the greatest battles of the war and had a total of 41,268 cases hospitalized.[728] Highly mobile, the division moved forty-one times throughout its wartime service and some of its units moved much more than that.[729] According to the division history, at the Côte de Châtillon the 42nd was to "see defeat face to face but instead of yielding it grimly, hung on even though ultimate success seem[ed] impossible."[730] It succeeded where other divisions had failed, and its efforts helped expedite the war's conclusion.

The three American divisions that tried to take the Côte de Châtillon—the 35th, 1st, and 42nd—had a unique story. The 35th was a poorly trained National Guard division of green soldiers under mediocre officers. The 1st was the best of the Regular Army. The 42nd was a well-trained, combat-experienced National Guard division, hand-picked from the best National Guard units. It had well-trained company and field grade officers answering mostly to West Pointers. These three divisions, which included the absolute best and worst of American citizenry volunteering and being drafted to fight, epitomize the mixed results of the US Army in France in 1918.

The book's core research comes from primary sources. The army archives openly record cowardice. Large numbers of soldiers went AWOL (Absent Without Leave), even while battles were taking place. Entire platoons disappeared for days at a time, wandering in safe places under the pretense of soldiering. Some soldiers ignored orders, and others sometimes failed to salute or otherwise follow the regulations of military courtesy — unforgivable sins for those striving to maintain discipline and order. Soldiers in lax National Guard units often neglected customs such as saluting their superiors, especially officers from their home towns. Some officers proved incompetent and failed in their duty without being held accountable. Command sent thousands of all ranks to the rear for reassignment, a disruptive and costly process, and some culprits were sent home. Total mental and physical exhaustion, the absence of hot food, and little or no rest sometimes broke even the best soldiers. Malingering could become a way of life for personnel at the margins. Conquering damaging behavior could require harsh measures, such as striking or physically hurting a soldier.

Cowardice aside, the biggest question remains unanswered. What inspired the heroism of the cold, tired, and vermin-ridden men who remained steadfast? Why did so many from simple farm, factory and immigrant backgrounds soldier on with distinction from one combat to the next? They, too, were often physically and mentally exhausted. What drove those men who constantly obeyed orders that put them into extreme danger?

All combat soldiers knew about misbehavior and insubordination. Some behaved terribly and some nobly, but little was said when the troops came home. In my opinion, the non-combatants, who constituted most of the last American soldiers arriving in France, had no war stories to tell. Their silence seemed convincing proof of their heroism to the civilians and family members who knew nothing about what they had done in the war. Likewise, those who experienced combat tended to go silent. A story of heroism could be misconstrued and dismissed as bragging. Those who returned with physical disabilities or shell shock, now better understood as PTSD, usually said little or nothing, and disabilities, alcoholism, and suicides sealed their stories within.

The Americans who fought on European soil returned to the United States with a different outlook on life. Those who had seen combat were, in fact, different; many were unable to readjust to the life they had known before, and they returned to a different country than the one they left. Their fellow citizens viewed them differently, as all faced daily life and changes like prohibition, women's suffrage, and a twentieth century more complicated in every way.

Men who would continue to play an important role in US history learned from the failure of the peace process. It allowed them some twenty years later to plan successfully for the aftermath of WWII. Working with other leaders, they recognized the mistake of not defeating Germany on its own soil, they developed the Marshall Plan to avoid another Depression, and they successfully created the United Nations from the lessons of the failed League of Nations.

The soldiers who fought in Europe in 1918 brought the United States to world leadership and gave birth to the American Century. Their story is part of our heritage.

AFTERWORD

Aftermath

The Musarde Farm occupied by German soldiers, like the nearby
Tuilerie Farm, 1915.

The full cost of WWI—psychological, physical, and financial—
may never be fully tallied. Countless lives were reshaped during the
years of conflict and their aftermath. For those who lived near battle
sites, life would never be the same.

Marguerite de Pouilly's unpublished memoir, excerpted in the
following pages, reflects the carefree pre-war days of early 1914. De
Pouilly, born in 1902, lived with her family in their ancestral home in
the Argonne, and her memoirs reflect initial excitement over seeing
big, dramatic military maneuvers. The home, named the Chateau de
Cornay, had come into the family in 1502 when Henri de Pouilly
married Jeanne de Granpré. In 1914 the castle was owned by Jean de
Pouilly, an artist and sculptor whose father, a veteran of the Franco-
Prussian War, died from his wounds when Jean was quite young. [731]

However, the summer brought many changes, and by the end of July, everyone was talking about war. The Pouilly family's German housekeeper returned to her native country, and eventually the war broke out. The Pouilly family fled the Argonne during the war, taking refuge in Belgium with Marguerite's mother's family, the Lejeune de Schiervel family. Their village and home were occupied by German troops until liberated by Americans. In the excerpt that follows, de Pouilly describes returning home for the first time after the war and grappling with the area's devastation.

Cornay, November 10, 1918.

A French family returns home to the Argonne, Easter 1919

The train from Sedan took several hours to cover 50 kilometers. [732] It was our first look at the landscape of these "devastated regions" that was going to be ours for years to come. The land was fallow and yellow from the residual of poison gas. Villages were disemboweled, trees shredded with grape shot and fields covered with shell holes…

Americans reigned supreme at Dun. The few locals looked

American with women in dresses fashioned from US Army blankets and men in old olive drab uniforms. My father was at the station in a kind of covered truck, donated by the Americans…They were starting to build their large cemetery, digging up their dead all along our route. It was a frightful spectacle that marked us for years to come…

After Romagne, we crossed what was left of the woods there. From afar we saw the broken roofs of Tuilerie Farm in the distance. We stood in the corner of the Kriemhilde line with nothing but shell holes, barbed wire, blockhouses and an excoriating odor given off by corpses. The Americans searching for their own dead had much to do. They left the Germans and horses to rot on the spot….

Reaching a hill beyond Sommerance, we saw the tree of Martincourt still standing, and the green stain of the first wheat sown by my father. Evening was falling, and we were very moved. It had taken us about four hours at the slow paces of the exhausted horses to cover about 20 kilometers. It took another hour of walking to reach the plank crossing that replaced the bridge at Saint-Juvin…The trails were unknown to us as the Germans had totally changed the topography. Finally, we arrived at Martincourt Farm. Stables and barn were burned but the house stood.

The François family of eight was cramped into two rooms of the house that was still standing. After dinner we left them and walked to Cornay. We found our poor house with torn doors, missing tiles and only half the windows. It was a gaping shell of ruins…

Our walk on the next day left an impression of total desolation and abandonment. There was no bell tower in the church and part of choir and the sacristy had fallen in our courtyard. There were only a few houses left standing in the village, and very few people other than Americans. There were deep bunkers, with huge piles of ammunition and equipment of all kinds. There were no roads, no big trees, not a bird, only hastily dug burial sites everywhere with Germans half dug up….

After Easter Mass at Grandpré, Madame Francois found a way to serve pies and coffee, a gift from the Americans. The Vanderesse family from the Tuilerie Farm on the Kriemhilde line were returning with their three sons to be able to claim compensation for dead livestock. Only a piece of wall of the farm could be seen in the distance. We had to go and see what had happened there. It was horrible. Nothing had been touched since the Armistice, lines and lines of barbed wire covered the fields and trenches were everywhere. As if by miracle, a part of Tuilerie Farm stood. In the courtyard were ten rotted corpses with as many in the garden and along the hedges. Dead horses stank up the air and the smell could not be overpowered. We gave up that attempt to reoccupy the farm...

NOTES

[1] Douglas MacArthur, *Reminiscences*, 66. French and American military texts and maps use the French word *cote* to refer to a hill and give its altitude. Cote and hill appear interchangeably in the sources. When presented with an accent, *côte* refers to the hill rather than the elevation.

[2] Nimrod T. Frazer, *Send the Alabamians*.

[3] Clair Kenamore, *From Vauquois Hill*, 87.

[4] Frédéric Guelton, "Les opérations," 44.

[5] *United States in World War I*, Vol. I, XX.

[6] Hélène Harter, *Les Etats-Unis*, 331.

[7] *United States in World War I*, Vol. I, XIX.

[8] American Battle Monuments Commission (hereafter cited as ABMC), *35th Division*, 11.

[9] Francis J. Reynolds, *Story*, 220.

[10] Henry J. Reilly, *Americans All*, 658-659.

[11] Most of these papers have recently been digitized and can be found at http://www.benning.army.mil/library/content/Virtual/Donovanpapers/wwi/.

[12] According to Louis Brouillon, "Under the French monarchy, the Argonne was divided between Champagne and Lorraine; after the Revolution, it was parceled in three pieces and given to the departments of Marne, Meuse, and Ardennes." (Brouillon, *L'Argonne*, 1, translated by Monique Seefried.) For additional information, see Douglas W. Johnson, *Battlefields*, 345 and fig. 78.

[13] Edward G. Lengel, ed., *Companion to the Meuse-Argonne*, 2.

[14] Jean-Noël Jeanneney, *Jours de Guerre*, 459.

[15] Walter Goerlitz, ed., *Kaiser and his Court*, 384.

[16] John S. D. Eisenhower, *Yanks*, 245.

[17] Gary Mead, *Doughboys*, 291.

[18] Mitchell Yockelson, *Forty-Seven Days*, 80.

[19] Robert Lee Bullard in collaboration with Earl Reeves, *American Soldiers Also Fought*, 92.

[20] Michael A. Eggleston, *5th Marine Regiment*, 91.

[21] Robert H. Ferrell, *Question of MacArthur's Reputation*, 1-2.

[22] Barnwell R. Legge, *1st Division*, 12. A native of Charleston, South Carolina, and graduate of The Citadel, Legge also rose to distinction in World War II after becoming a military attaché to Switzerland in 1939.

[23] John J. Pershing, *Final Report*, 43.

[24] William J. Abbot, *United States*, 21.

[25] Kenamore, *From Vauquois Hill*, 76.

[26] Donald Kyler, *Thoughts & Memories*, 105.

[27] Johnson, *Battlefields*, 337.

[28] Edward G. Lengel, *To Conquer Hell*, 69.

[29] James G. Harbord, *American Army in France*, 430-431.

[30] Charles Pelot Summerall, *Way of Duty*, 137.

[31] Mead, *Doughboys*, 299.

[32] Lengel, *To Conquer Hell*, 69.

[33] ABMC, *35th Division*, 9.

[34] Eisenhower, *Yanks*, 240.

[35] NARA, RG 120, Box 3381, Folder 112.08, Field Order No 20, First U.S. Army, September 20, 1918.

[36] Eisenhower, *Yanks*, 210.

[37] Pershing, *Final Report*, 43.

[38] Paul F. Braim, *Test of Battle*, 74.

[39] Robert E. Bruce, *Fraternity of Arms*, 271.

[40] Lengel, *To Conquer Hell*, 52.

[41] John V. Stark, *3rd Battalion*, 6.

[42] Stark, 2.

[43] Kenamore, *From Vauquois Hill*, 76

[44] Robert H. Ferrell, *Collapse at Meuse-Argonne*, 18; Lengel, *To Conquer Hell*, 108.

[45] A. Ward Gillette, *Historical Tactical Study*, 8.

[46] Gillette, 8.

[47] Ferrell, *Collapse at Meuse–Argonne*, 4.

[48] ABMC, *35th Division*, 11.

[49] Lengel, *To Conquer Hell*, 85.

[50] Stark, *3rd Battalion*, 6.

[51] Robert H. Ferrell, *America's Deadliest Battle*, 44.

[52] C. Douglas Sterner, ed., *Citations for Awards of The Distinguished Service Cross* (hereafter cited as *CADSC*), III, 324; Kenamore, *From Vauquois Hill*, 87.

[53] John J. Pershing, *My Experiences*, 290.

[54] Field Order 20 is covered in Annex 10 (Battle Instruction, Operation Z) Ligny-en-Barrois, 1st Army, September 18, 1918, 116, United States Army in the World War 1917-1919, Vol. 9, Military Operations of the American Expeditionary Forces.

[55] John S. D. Eisenhower, *Yanks*, 213.

[56] Matthias Strohn, ed., *World War I Companion*, 200.

[57] Lengel, *To Conquer Hell*, 86.

[58] Lengel, *To Conquer Hell*, 108.

[59] Pershing, *My Experiences*, 296.

[60] Lengel, *To Conquer Hell*, 114.

[61] Kenamore, *From Vauquois Hill*, 98.

[62] Sterner, *CADSC*, IV, 99.

[63] Sterner, II, 275-276. English received the DSC for this action. He received a DSC (First Oak Leaf Cluster) on October 4 for a reconnaissance mission, during which he was killed.

[64] Sterner, II, 340-341.

[65] Sterner, III, 308; ABMC, *35th Division*, 13.

[66] Sterner, III, 122.

[67] Sterner, IV, 53.

[68] Sterner, IV, 131.

[69] Sterner, III, 116.

[70] Kenamore, *From Vauquois Hill*, 112.

[71] *American Decorations*, 119.

[72] Sterner, *CADSC*, IV, 147.

[73] Sterner, III, 360-361.

[74] ABMC, *35th Division*, 14.

[75] Lengel, *To Conquer Hell*, 111.

[76] Colonel Castle file, Special Collections at the USMA Collection at West Point; H.W. Crocker, *Yanks are Coming*, 200.

[77] Lengel, *To Conquer Hell*, 111.

[78] Ferrell, *Collapse at Meuse-Argonne*, 28-39; Eisenhower, *Yanks*, 215. Patton would come back to fight in this area during WWII and would even establish his headquarters at the foot of the Côte de Châtillon, the 35th Division's objective in WWI.

[79] *Monographs of the World War*, 577; Kenamore, *From Vauquois Hill*, 137.

[80] Eisenhower, *Yanks*, 210.

[81] Kennamore, *From Vauquois Hill*, 93.

[82] Lengel, *To Conquer Hell*, 112.

[83] Reilly, *Americans All*, 605.

[84] Bullard with Reeves, *American Soldiers Also Fought*, 94.

[85] Hunter Liggett, *Commanding an American Army*, 80.

[86] ABMC, *35th Division*, 10; James Scott Wheeler, *Big Red One*, 78.

[87] John C. Lenahan, *Analysis to the 35th*, 22.

[88] Lengel, *To Conquer Hell*, 115.

[89] ABMC, *American Armies and Battlefields*, 173.

[90] Frank E. Bonney, *Operations of the Thirty-Fifth*, 9.

[91] Kenamore, *From Vauquois Hill*, 148.

[92] Ferrell, *Collapse at Meuse-Argonne*, 64-66.

[93] Ferrell, 47.

[94] Reilly, *Americans All*, 605; William W. Wright, *Meuse Argonne Diary*, 45.

[95] Bonney, *Operations of the Thirty-Fifth*, 14.

[96] Sterner, *CADSC*, III, 311.

[97] Sterner, IV, 105.

[98] Lenahan, *Analysis to the 35th*, 30.

[99] ABMC, *35th Division*, 16.

[100] ABMC, *American Armies and Battlefields*, 175.

[101] Lenahan, *Analysis to the 35th*, 31.

[102] Ferrell, *Collapse at Meuse-Argonne*, IX.

[103] Ferrell, 56-59; Lenahan, *Analysis to the 35th*, 31.

[104] Sterner, IV, 223.

[105] Sterner, III, 86.

[106] Sterner, IV, 70.

[107] Sterner, III, 287.

[108] Sterner, II, 233.

[109] Sterner, II, 252.

[110] Sterner, III, 163.

[111] Ferrell, *Collapse at Meuse-Argonne*, 52.

[112] Lenahan, *Analysis to the 35th*, 31.

[113] Reilly, *Americans All*, 607.

[114] *Monographs of the World War*, 504-517; *History of the First Division*, 183.

[115] ABMC, *35th Division*, 17.

[116] Bonney, *Operations of the Thirty-Fifth*, 33.

[117] B. F. Caffey, *Operations of the 1st*, 18.

[118] Ferrell, *Collapse at Meuse-Argonne*, 83.

[119] Lenahan, *Analysis to the 35th*, 32.

[120] Sterner, *CADSC*, III, 308; ABMC, *35th Division*, 18.

[121] ABMC, 10.

[122] Ferrell, *Question of MacArthur's Reputation*, 2.

[123] ABMC, *American Armies and Battlefields*, 175.

[124] Ferrell, *Collapse at Meuse-Argonne*, 83-84.

[125] Lenahan, *Analysis to the 35th*, 35.

[126] ABMC, *35th Division*, 19.

[127] ABMC, 10.

[128] Stark, *3rd Battalion*, 15.

[129] Wheeler, *The Big Red One*, 83.

[130] Sterner, *CADSC*, III, 105.

[131] Bonney, *Operations of the Thirty-Fifth*, 10.

[132] Stark, *3rd Battalion*, 13.

[133] Strohn, *World War I Companion*, 206-207.

[134] Ferrell, *Collapse at Meuse-Argonne*, 62-63.

[135] Ferrell, *Question of MacArthur's Reputation*, 2.

[136] Wheeler, *The Big Red One*, 82.

[137] Mark Ethan Grotelueschen, *AEF Way of War*, 132.

[138] Ferrell, *Collapse in the Meuse-Argonne*, 9.

[139] Reilly, *Americans All*, 603.

[140] Bullard with Reeves, *American Soldiers Also Fought*, 99.

[141] Frederick Palmer, *Our Greatest Battle*, 192.

[142] Letter from Harry Truman to Bess Truman, October 6, 1918, https://www.trumanlibrary.org/whistlestop/study_collections/ww1/documents/index.php?documentdate=1918-10-06&documentid=1-17&pagenumber=1.

[143] Yockelson, *Forty-Seven Days*, 101.

[144] Pershing, *My Experiences*, 299.

[145] Bruce, *Fraternity of Arms*, 271.

[146] *History of the First Division*, 183.

[147] Ferrell, *America's Deadliest Battle*, 94.

[148] Wheeler, *Big Red One*, 80.

[149] ABMC, *35th Division*, 10.

[150] Lengel, *To Conquer Hell*, 212.

[151] Mark D. Van Ells, *America and World War I*, 207.

[152] Grotelueschen, *AEF Way of War*, 125.

[153] Eisenhower, *Yanks*, 223.

[154] Martin Hogan, *Shamrock Battalion*, 232-233.

[155] The Fifth Army Corps – AEF during the Meuse-Argonne Operation AC

No. 19937, Jan 24, 1919 – Second Phase, 6. *Stellung* means station in German.

156 Nancy Gentile Ford, *Americans All*, 145.

157 George C. Marshall. *Memoirs of my Services*, 8.

158 Henry Russell Miller, *First Division*, 3-4.

159 AMHI, Veterans Survey, Earl R. Poorbaugh, Corporal, 26th Infantry Regiment, First Division.

160 Legge, *1st Division*, 13.

161 *Order of Battle*, Vol. 2, 5-13.

162 Lyman S. Frasier, *Operations*, 2.

163 Yockelson, *Forty-Seven Days*, 123.

164 Caffey, *Operations of the 1st*, 6.

165 Herbert B. McHenry, *As A Private*, 38-42.

166 Frasier, *Operations*, 3.

167 F. S. Doll, *1st Division, Meuse-Argonne*, 2.

168 Ralph E. McLain, *Organization and Operations*, 1.

169 Doll, *1st Division, Meuse-Argonne*, 2.

170 Caffey, *Operations of the 1st*, 3.

171 "Horse lines" is a colloquialism for *chevaux de frise*, defensive barriers used to plug gaps in the wire.

172 Legge, *1st Division*, 4.

173 Caffey, *Operations of the 1st*, 6.

174 *History of the First Division*, 176.

175 *History of the 1st Division*, 174; Caffey, *Operations of the 1st*, 5.

176 Wheeler, *Big Red One*, 82.

177 NARA, RG 165, German Military Records 1917-1919, Entry 320, quotation translated from original German, Folder 3, Copy 1, Copies of entries in the War Day Book of the Argonne Group, Kriegstagebuch mit Anlagen des Generalkommandos z.b.V. 58, 12.

178 Ben Chastaine, *History of the 18th*, 89.

179 The region includes many forests that cover the Argonne plateau. A historical region of France, the Argonne extends beyond the Argonne plateau and includes such towns as Gesnes-en-Argonne, Givry-en-Argonne, and Montfaucon-en-Argonne. Before the French Revolution the Argonne was located partly in Champagne and partly in Lorraine. It was divided after the Revolution between the departments of the Marne, the Meuse, and the Ardennes.

180 Wheeler, *Big Red One*, 82-85.

[181] Summaries, Meuse - - Argonne, Sept.21, 1918 – Nov. 20, 1918, Summary of Intelligence September 30, 1918.

[182] Grotelueschen, *AEF Way of War*, 140.

[183] *History of the First Division*, 196.

[184] Leonard R. Boyd, *Operations*, 1.

[185] Legge, *1st Division*, 555.

[186] Caffey, *Operations of the 1st*, 6.

[187] *History of the First Division*, 178.

[188] Eisenhower, *Yanks*, 231.

[189] *History of the First Division*, 182.

[190] Wheeler, *Big Red One*, 84.

[191] Chastaine, *History of the 18th*, 89.

[192] Wheeler, *Big Red One*, 83.

[193] Caffey, *Operations of the 1st*, 9; Peter L. Belmonte, *Days of Perfect Hell*, 37.

[194] NARA, ABMC Correspondence with Division Officers, July 1, 1936, Major Barnwell R. Legge.

[195] Sterner, *CADSC*, II, 14.

[196] Sterner, III, 112.

[197] Sterner, III, 81.

[198] Sterner, II, 326-327.

[199] Sterner, III, 64.

[200] Sterner, III, 122.

[201] Sterner, II, 287.

[202] Sterner, III, 5-6.

[203] Sterner, II, 348.

[204] Bullard with Reeves, *American Soldiers Also Fought*, 5.

[205] Belmonte, *Days of Perfect Hell*, 36.

[206] Thousands of trees have also been planted since 1918, and all have been cared for by the French ONF.

[207] Wheeler, *Big Red One*, 82; Reilly, *Americans All*, 611.

[208] James Metcalf, *Operations*, 543.

[209] *History of the First Division*, 204.

[210] Belmonte, *Days of Perfect Hell*, 37.

[211] *History of The First Division*, 184.

[212] M. S. Eddy, *Critical Analysis*, 7.

[213] Eddy, 6-8.

[214] Caffey, *Operations of the 1st*, 11.

[215] Field Order No. 49, the Artillery Attack Order.

[216] McHenry, *As a Private*, 38-49.

[217] Caffey, *Operations*, 11.

[218] Caffey, 12.

[219] Caffey, 11.

[220] *History of the 2nd*, 36.

[221] Eisenhower, *Yanks*, 232.

[222] Caffey, *Operations of the 1st*, 11.

[223] Sterner, *CADSC*, IV, 109.

[224] Sterner, II, 179.

[225] Sterner, III, 341-342.

[226] Sterner, II, 28.

[227] *History of the First Division*, 187.

[228] *History of the First Division*, 187.

[229] Sterner, *CADSC*, III, 207.

[230] Kyler, *Thoughts & Memories*, 108.

[231] Sterner, *CADSC*, IV, 73.

[232] Sterner, III, 209.

[233] Sterner, III, 92.

[234] Sterner, III, 141.

[235] Sterner, II, 95.

[236] Sterner, II, 13.

[237] *History of the First Division*, 182.

[238] Eddy, *Critical Analysis*, 9.

[239] *History of the 2nd*, 36; Reilly, *Americans All*, 623.

[240] Kyler, *Thoughts & Memories*, 110.

[241] Sterner, *CADSC*, III, 242.

[242] Earl H. Weed, *Story of The Sixteenth*; Hartzell, *Meuse-Argonne Battle*, 30-31; *History of the First Division*, 189.

[243] Kyler, *Thoughts & Memories*, 106.

[244] Sterner, *CADSC*, II, 112.

[245] Sterner, IV, 48.

[246] Sterner, IV, 74.

[247] Sterner, IV, 57.

[248] Sterner, III, 124.

[249] Sterner, II, 335.

[250] Legge, *1st Division,* 24.

[251] Sterner, *CADSC,* IV, 208. Wells received a DSC (First Oak Leaf Cluster) for his actions. This was his second such award, as he had received a DSC for his actions near Buzancy in July.

[252] Wheeler, *Big Red One,* 86.

[253] *History of The First Division,* 189.

[254] *History of the First Division,* 190.

[255] *History of the First Division,* 189.

[256] Kyler, *Thoughts & Memories,* 112.

[257] AMHI, *Casualties, Meuse-Argonne Offensive,* 95.

[258] Chastaine, *History of the 18th,* 91.

[259] Sterner, *CADSC,* II, 156.

[260] Sterner, II, 11.

[261] Sterner, II, 192.

[262] Field Message, NARA, 201-32.16.

[263] Chastaine, *History of the 18th U.S. Infantry,* 92.

[264] Wheeler, *Big Red One,* 87.

[265] Caffey, *Operations of the 1st,* 15.

[266] Caffey, 12.

[267] Wheeler, *Big Red One,* 84.

[268] Chastaine, *History of the 18th,* 91.

[269] Caffey, *Operations of the 1st,* 13.

[270] Wheeler, *Big Red One,* 84.

[271] George R. F. Cornish, *First Division US,* 35-36.

[272] *History of the First Division,* 194.

[273] Legge, *1st Division,* 555-559.

[274] Eisenhower, *Yanks,* 232.

[275] Sterner, *CADSC,* IV, 250.

[276] Frasier, *Operations,* 10.

[277] Frasier, 11-12.

[278] Sterner, *CADSC,* III, 185.

[279] Frasier, *Operations,* 14.

[280] Sterner, *CADSC,* II, 52.

[281] Sterner, II, 305.

[282] Sterner, II, 238.

[283] Sterner, III, 311.

[284] Sterner, III, 291.

[285] Sterner, II, 264.

[286] Sterner, II, 211.

[287] Stephen L. Bowman, *Century of Valor*, 46.

[288] *History of the First Division*, 185.

[289] *History of the First Division*, 191-193.

[290] Sterner, *CADSC*, III, 149.

[291] *American Decorations*, 74.

[292] Caffey, *Operations of the 1st*, 22.

[293] Sterner, *CADSC*, II, 321 & 324; *CADSC*, III, 126.

[294] Belmonte, *Days of Perfect Hell*, 179.

[295] Frasier, *Operations*, 9.

[296] Cornish, *First Division*, 35-36; *History of the First Division*, 53, 193.

[297] Charles B. Fullerton, *Twenty-Sixth Infantry*, 65, 79.

[298] William A. Mansfield, *Diary of a Shavetail*.

[299] Frasier, *Operations*, 6.

[300] Caffey, *Operations of the 1st*, 13.

[301] *History of the First Division*, 187.

[302] Caffey, *Operations of the 1st*, 20.

[303] Legge, *1st Division*, 18.

[304] Wheeler, *Big Red One*, 84-87.

[305] *History of the First Division*, 193.

[306] Frasier, *Operations*, 9; Boyd, *Operations*, 4.

[307] Frasier, 10.

[308] Sterner, *CADSC*, II, 344.

[309] Fullerton, *Twenty-Sixth Infantry*, 66.

[310] Caffey, *Operations of the First*, 16.

[311] Summerall, *Way of Duty*, 138.

[312] Kyler, *Thoughts & Memories*, 113-115.

[313] Caffey, *Operations of the 1st*, 14.

[314] Legge, *1st Division*, 19.

[315] Caffey, *Operations of the 1st*, 4.

[316] *History of the 1st Division*, 204.

[317] NARA, *original German folder* 1-810-335, 25.

[318] Sterner, *CADSC*, III, 178.

[319] Sterner, II, 195.

[320] Sterner, IV, 159.

321 NARA, *original German folder* 1-810-335, 25.

322 Caffey, *Operations of the 1st,* 12.

323 *American Decorations,* 30; Bowman, *A Century of Valor,* 47.

324 Sterner, *CADSC,* III, 309.

325 Sterner, III, 168.

326 Sterner, III, 301.

327 Sterner, II, 46.

328 Sterner, IV, 128.

329 Sterner, IV, 197.

330 Sterner, II, 208.

331 Sterner, III, 327.

332 Sterner, IV, 147.

333 Sterner, II, 157-158.

334 Sterner, IV, 198-199.

335 Sterner, IV, 134.

336 Sterner, II, 130.

337 AMHI, *Letter from Captain William Haselton,* Oct.6, 1918, Correspondence, First Division Headquarters.

338 Frasier, *Operations,* 11.

339 George J. Forster, *Operations of the 37mm,* 10.

340 Frasier, *Operations,* 12.

341 Frasier, 15.

342 Frasier, 13.

343 Frasier, 14.

344 Frasier, 13.

345 Caffey, *Operations of the 1st,* 16-18.

346 Frasier, *Operations,* 16.

347 Forster, *Operations of the 27mm,* 15.

348 Forster, 13.

349 Despite the tensions that sometimes arose over division collaboration, such collaboration soon led to a major unexpected event that helped straighten the American line and drive a wedge into the German position. Most importantly, it prevented a battle later. Corps had ordered Summerall to assist the 32nd Division on its right. To do so, he ordered the commanding officer of the 16th Infantry battalion to send a patrol towards Cote 269. After the patrol reported that the hill was not occupied, a subsequent patrol of twenty-four men secured it. The brigade commander

then sent two rifle companies from the 26th Infantry with instructions to capture the Bois de Moncy and Cote 269. While taking Cote 269, they took out nine Germans and nine machine guns. This success in taking 269 without a major attack surprised everyone, and it was the only prominent terrain feature between the Exermont Ravine and the Côte de Châtillon that fell to the Americans so easily.

[350] Reilly, *Americans All*, 623.

[351] Frasier, *Operations*, 16

[352] Frasier, 29; Wheeler, *Big Red One*, 87.

[353] Belmonte, *Days of Perfect Hell*, 70.

[354] Sterner, *CADSC*, III, 226.

[355] Sterner, II, 256.

[356] NARA RG 120 Records of Combat Divisions 1918-1919 42nd Division, Box 41 ARC 10 301641 Entry NM-911241; Frasier, *Operations*, 15.

[357] McHenry, *As A Private*, 38-42.

[358] Frasier, *Operations*, 18.

[359] Frasier, 18-19.

[360] Frasier, 19.

[361] Frasier, 30-31.

[362] Frasier, 19.

[363] Frasier, 19.

[364] NARA, RG 120 Records of Combat Divisions 1918-1919 42nd Division, Box 41 ARC 10 301641 Entry NM-911241, 97.

[365] Frasier, *Operations*, 22.

[366] Frasier, 33.

[367] Frasier, 22.

[368] Frasier, 27.

[369] Frasier, 35.

[370] Sterner, *CADSC*, III, 221.

[371] Sterner, II, 232.

[372] Sterner, III, 363.

[373] Sterner, III, 186.

[374] Frasier, *Operations*, 34.

[375] Frasier, 28.

[376] Frasier, 24.

[377] Eddy, *Critical Analysis*, 35.

[378] Summerall, *Way of Duty*, 138.

[379] *History of the First Division*, 195.

[380] Wheeler, *Big Red One,* 88.

[381] Summerall, *Way of Duty,* 138.

[382] Frasier, *Operations,* 7, and "The 32ᴰ 'Red Arrow' Veteran Association," revised December 2017, http://www.32nd-division.org/history/ww1/32-ww1a.html.

[383] Field Message to 42nd Div. Headquarters, Oct. 7, 1918 confirming Brig. General Bamford's verbal order on October 7.

[384] Sterner, *CADSC*, II, 320.

[385] US Army AEF 1914.1918 1st Division World War Records V.X.V.

[386] Caffey, *Operations of the 1st*, 19.

[387] Legge, *1st Division,* 26.

[388] NARA, *Letter from C.D. Richards to ABMC* File 710.1-M/MA, Sept. 4, 1926.

[389] Sterner, *CADSC*, II, 90.

[390] Sterner, III, 162.

[391] Sterner, III, 133.

[392] Sterner, II, 94-95.

[393] Sterner, II, 212.

[394] Sterner, III, 208.

[395] Sterner, IV, 167.

[396] Sterner, IV, 154.

[397] Sterner, IV, 59.

[398] Sterner, II, 88.

[399] Sterner, III, 35-36.

[400] NARA *Memorandum for Chief of Staff, Headquarters*, 1st Division, 201-32.15.

[401] Sterner, *CADSC*, II, 253.

[402] Sterner, II, 25.

[403] Sterner, II, 280.

[404] Legge, *1st Division,* 27; Frasier, *Operations,* 28.

[405] Frasier, 28.

[406] Legge, *1st Division,* 27.

[407] Sterner, *CADSC*, II, 287.

[408] Frasier, *Operations,* 32.

[409] Frasier, 32.

[410] Frasier, 34.

[411] Boyd, *Operations,* 2.

[412] NARA, *Summaries, Meuse-Argonne, Sept. 21-Nov. 20. 1918*, First Division.

[413] Boyd, *Operations*, 2.

[414] Boyd, *Operations*, 10.

[415] Sterner, *CADSC*, II, 76.

[416] Legge, *1st Division*, 27.

[417] Boyd, *Operations*, 5.

[418] Frasier, *Operations*, 37-42.

[419] Sterner, *CADSC*, III, 251.

[420] Sterner, II, 240.

[421] Sterner, III, 338.

[422] Sterner, II, 65.

[423] Sterner, III, 172.

[424] NARA, *Summaries, Meuse-Argonne, Sept. 21-Nov. 20. 1918,* 1st Division.

[425] Reilly, *Americans All*, 613.

[426] Eisenhower, *Yanks*, 236.

[427] *American Decorations*, 121.

[428] Eisenhower, *Yanks*, 238.

[429] Yockelson, *Forty-Seven Days*, 240.

[430] Rod Parschall, *Defeat of Imperial Germany*, 189-191.

[431] Yockelson, *Forty-Seven Days*, 247.

[432] Millett, Allan R., *General, Robert L. Bullard*, 410.

[433] Sterner, *CADSC,* IV, 50.

[434] Sterner, II, 110.

[435] Sterner, IV, 224.

[436] Sterner, IV, 19-20.

[437] Sterner, IV, 121.

[438] Albert B. Helsley, *Operations of the Machine*, 31.

[439] Helsley, 40.

[440] *History of The First Division*, 203-4.

[441] Helsley, *Operations of the Machine*, 43.

[442] Reilly, *Americans All*, 621.

[443] Reilly, 624.

[444] Boyd, *Operations*, 2.

[445] *History of The First Division*, 195.

[446] Wheeler, *Big Red One*, 89.

[447] Sterner, *CADSC*, II, 63.

[448] Grotelueschen, *AEF Way of War*, 137.

[449] NARA, RG 120 *Records of Combat Divisions 1918-1919 42nd Division*, Box 41 ARC 10 301641 Entry NM-911241, 96.

[450] Boyd, *Operations*, 9.

[451] *History of the 1st Division*, 208.

[452] McHenry, *As A Private*, 48.

[453] Helsley, *Operations of the Machine*, 41-42.

[454] McHenry, *As A Private*, 48.

[455] Boyd, *Operations*, 3.

[456] Weed, *Story of the Sixteenth*.

[457] *History of the 1st Division*, 208.

[458] Boyd, *Operations*, 10.

[459] Helsley, *Operations of the Machine*, 47.

[460] Legge, *1st Division*, 29.

[461] Boyd, *Operations*, 10.

[462] Helsley, *Operations of the Machine*, 45- 47.

[463] Boyd, *Operations*, 20.

[464] Boyd, 16.

[465] Boyd, 20.

[466] Boyd, 13.

[467] Helsley, *Operations of the Machine*, 37.

[468] Sterner, *CSDSC*, II, 145.

[469] Sterner, IV, 177.

[470] Sterner, II, 273-274.

[471] Sterner, III, 123. Kimmel received a DSC (First Oak Leaf Cluster) for his actions; he had previously received a DSC for his service near Soissons in July.

[472] Sterner, III, 36.

[473] 1st Division Divisional Orders. General Orders number 58.

[474] Sterner, *CADSC*, II, 58.

[475] Sterner, IV, 254.

[476] Sterner, III, 354.

[477] Sterner, III, 341.

[478] Sterner, IV, 249.

[479] Sterner, III, 162.

[480] Sterner, II, 37.

[481] Sterner, II, 41-42.

[482] Boyd, *Operations*, 27.

[483] Sterner, *CADSC*, III, 300.

[484] Sterner, III, 179.

[485] Sterner, III, 197.

[486] Sterner, IV, 191.

[487] Steven E. Clay, *Blood and Sacrifice*, 114-115.

[488] Steven E. Clay, 114-115.

[489] AMHI, Army Services Experience Questionnaire, 1st Division, 2nd MG Battalion, Elvid B. Johnson.

[490] Grotelueschen, *AEF Way of War*, 137.

[491] Chastaine, *History of the 18th*, 96.

[492] Boyd, *Operations*, 20.

[493] Boyd, 23.

[494] Sterner, *CADSC*, IV, 128.

[495] Reilly, *Americans All*, 624.

[496] Summerall, *Way of Duty*, 139.

[497] Helsley, *Operations of the Machine*, 48.

[498] Summerall, *Way of Duty*, 139.

[499] Boyd, *Operations*, 1.

[500] Helsley *Operations of the Machine*, 37.

[501] Helsley, 53.

[502] Boyd, *Operations*, 21.

[503] Boyd, 80.

[504] Wheeler, *Big Red One*, 259. Like many of the Big Red One's mustangs he rose to high rank and service in World War II, becoming a Major General on March 12, 1943. Huebner succeeded Terry Allen as commander of the 1st Division (where he served with Theodore Roosevelt Jr. when Roosevelt was first the 26th Infantry commander and later the assistant division commander). He became commander of the division and prepared it to lead the invasion of Nazi-occupied Europe.

[505] *Story of The Twenty-Eighth*, 29.

[506] Belmonte, *Days of Perfect Hell*, 113.

[507] Frasier, *Operations*, 43.

[508] Frasier, 44.

[509] *History of the First Division*, 211.

[510] Frasier, *Operations*, 47.

[511] Boyd, *Operations*, 27.

[512] Chastaine, History of the 18th U.S. Infantry, 98.

513 Frasier, *Operations,* 46.

514 Frasier, 46.

515 Frasier, 49.

516 Sterner, *CADSC,* III, 177-178.

517 Sterner, III, 255-256.

518 Sterner, III, 324-325.

519 Sterner, III, 186.

520 Sterner, III, 293.

521 Reilly, *Americans All,* 624.

522 Legge, *1st Division, 32.*

523 NARA, Box 156.

524 Sterner, *CADSC,* IV, 48.

525 Forster, *Operations of the 37mm,* 19.

526 Summerall, *Way of Duty,* 141-143.

527 Ferrell, *America's Deadliest Battle,* 98.

528 Braim, *Test of Battle,* 126.

529 Wheeler, *Big Red One,* 88-89.

530 Reilly, *Americans All,* 625.

531 Field message, NARA 201-32.16.

532 Reilly, *Americans All,* 624.

533 Field message, NARA 201-32.16.

534 Sterner, *CADSC,* III, 361.

535 Sterner, III, 364.

536 Sterner, III, 312.

537 Sterner, IV, 92.

538 Eisenhower, *Yanks,* 250.

539 *First Division History,* 208.

540 Boyd, *Operations,* 30.

541 Frasier, *Operations,* 49.

542 Wheeler, *Big Red One,* 91.

543 Kyler, *Thoughts & Memories,* 115.

544 Kyler, 112-113.

545 *History of The First Division,* 208.

546 Summerall, *Way of Duty,* 141.

547 *History of the First Division,* XV.

548 John H. Taber, *Story of the 168th Infantry,* II, 155.

[549] Nick Lloyd, *Hundred Days*, 200.

[550] Lloyd, 200.

[551] Reilly, *Americans All*, 624.

[552] Wheeler, *Big Red One*, 86-91.

[553] Ann Cipriano Venzon, ed. *United States*, 118.

[554] Reilly, *Americans All*, 647.

[555] Taber, *Story of the 168th Infantry*, II, 161.

[556] As recorded in *Journal des Marches et Opérations*, Novembre 1917–Janvier 1919, 42e DIUS Mission Française, SHD/DAT.

[557] Braim, *Test of Battle*, 126.

[558] Amerine, *Alabama's Own in France*, 189.

[559] Amerine, 190.

[560] Edward R. Wren, *Letters*, October 8, 1918.

[561] Bullard with Reeves, *American Soldiers Also Fought*, 100.

[562] Wright, *Meuse Argonne Diary*, 1.

[563] R. M. Cheseldine, *Ohio in the Rainbow*, 245.

[564] Lawrence O. Stewart, *Rainbow Bright*, 119.

[565] James H. Hallas, *Doughboy War*, 278-279.

[566] Francis P. Duffy, *Father Duffy's Story*, 62.

[567] Hallas, *Doughboy War*, 278-279.

[568] Reilly, *Americans All*, 630-632.

[569] Cheseldine, *Ohio in the Rainbow*, 247.

[570] Cheseldine, 246.

[571] Cheseldine, 249.

[572] Cheseldine, 245-246.

[573] Amerine, *Alabama's Own in France*, 191.

[574] Taber, *Story of the 168th*, II, 156-160.

[575] Taber, II, 156-160.

[576] Taber, II, 208.

[577] Taber, II, 160.

[578] Reilly, *Americans All*, 668.

[579] Eskil I. Bjork, *Harness & Hitch*, 173.

[580] Bjork, 178.

[581] Bjork, 178.

[582] Bjork, 199.

[583] Amerine, *Alabama's Own in France*, 191.

[584] Lengel, *To Conquer Hell*, 308.

[585] Reilly, *Americans All*, 644.

[586] Amerine, *Alabama's Own in France*, 191.

[587] NARA, RG 120, Box 41, Records 42nd Division, Letter from the Commanding General, George G. Gatley to the Commanding General 42nd Division, October 17, 1918.

[588] Cheseldine, *Ohio in the Rainbow*, 249.

[589] Amerine, *Alabama's Own in France*, 193.

[590] Louis L. Collins, *History of the 151st*, 138.

[591] Taber, *Story of the 168th*, II, 160.

[592] ABMC File 714.2-M/MA, February 5, 1926 Summary of Operations, 42nd Division in Meuse Argonne on October 12, 1918, 2.

[593] Elmer Frank Straub, *Sergeant's Diary*, 195.

[594] Leslie Langille, *Men of the Rainbow*, 158.

[595] Collins, *History of the 151st*, 146.

[596] Reilly, *Americans All*, 648.

[597] Reilly, 646.

[598] Reilly, 622.

[599] Reilly, 649.

[600] Collins, *History of the 151st*, 146.

[601] ABMC, 165th Infantry, 42nd Division, Box 232, RG 117.

[602] David G. Fivecoat, *Fine Conduct Under Fire*, 77-80.

[603] Duffy, *Father Duffy's Story*, 266-268.

[604] Reilly, *Americans All*, 653.

[605] Lengel, *To Conquer Hell*, 353.

[606] Reilly, *Americans All*, 657.

[607] ABMC File 714.2-M/MA, October 25, 1926 Summary of Operations, 42nd Division in Meuse Argonne, I/165 Roderick J. Hutcheson, Formerly 2nd Lieutenant.

[608] Hallas, *Doughboy War*, 279.

[609] Ferrell, *Question of MacArthur's Reputation*, 23.

[610] Royal Little Correspondence with ABMC November 26, 1926, MAMA, RG-15, Box 75, Folder 5.

[611] Reilly, *Americans All*, 690.

[612] MAMA, 165th Inf, 42nd Div, box 232, BMC, RG 117 Letter Henry A. Bootz to the Commandant, The Infantry School, considered in final check July 21, 1930.

[613] Collins, *History of the 151st*, 147.

[614] Fivecoat, *Fine Conduct Under Fire*, 78.

[615] The English soldiers had nicknamed the Germans "Jerry" due to the shape of their helmets, which were shaped like chamber pots. In English slang, chamber pots are referred to as "jerries."

[616] Letter from Dalton Hayes to his mother from Base Hospital 61, October 22, 1918. Rutherford B. Hayes Presidential Library.

[617] Sterner, *CADSC*, IV, 234.

[618] Sterner, IV, 25.

[619] Sterner, IV, 192-193.

[620] Sterner, III, 308.

[621] *American Decorations*, 27.

[622] Sterner, *CADSC*, III, 67-68.

[623] Sterner, IV, 218.

[624] Cheseldine, *Ohio in the Rainbow*, 249.

[625] Sterner, *CADSC* II, 251.

[626] Cheseldine, *Ohio in the Rainbow*, 247.

[627] Cheseldine, 252.

[628] Sterner, III, 52.

[629] War Diary of the 166th Infantry, reported verbatim in Cheseldine, *Ohio in the Rainbow*, 250-253.

[630] Cheseldine, 251.

[631] Cheseldine, 250.

[632] Report of Activities, 149th Field Artillery, April 14-15, 1918, 1st Lieutenant G. L. Lawrence, Intelligence Officer.

[633] ABMC file 714.2-M/MA, October 30, 1926, I Company, 166, 42nd Division, Meuse Argonne Operations, Letter #5, Virgil R. Peck.

[634] Cheseldine, *Ohio in the Rainbow*, 250.

[635] Cheseldine, 250.

[636] Sterner, *CADSC*, II, 295.

[637] ABMC file 714.2-M/MA, Feb. 5, 1926, 5.

[638] Cheseldine, *Ohio in the Rainbow*, 251.

[639] War Diary of the 166th Infantry, reported verbatim in Cheseldine, 250-253.

[640] Summerall, *Way of Duty*, 144.

[641] Collins, *History of the 151st*, 147.

[642] Sterner, *CADSC*, IV, 19.

[643] Sterner, III, 9-10.

[644] Sterner, III, 311.

[645] Sterner, III, 105-106.

[646] Sterner, II, 199.

[647] Sterner, IV, 156.

[648] Sterner, II, 119.

[649] Sterner, II, 295-296.

[650] Fivecoat, *Fine Conduct Under Fire*, 79.

[651] Reilly, *Americans All*, 696

[652] Sterner, *CADSC*, III, 310.

[653] Reilly, *Americans All*, 646

[654] Duffy, *Father Duffy's Story*, 270.

[655] Sterner, *CADSC*, II, 36.

[656] Sterner, IV, 186.

[657] Sterner, II, 135.

[658] Sterner, II, 173.

[659] Sterner, IV, 14.

[660] Sterner, II, 317.

[661] ABMC File A-714.2-M/MA,November 16, 1926, Machine Gun Company, 165th 42nd Division in Meuse Argonne, I/165. R.B. DeLacour, Lt. Res.

[662] Sterner, *CADSC*, II, 128.

[663] Duffy, *Father Duffy's Story*, 278.

[664] Major Henry Bootz, Correspondence with ABMC, April 5, 1930, 3rd Ind., MAMA, RG-15, Box 35-41, Folder 5.

[665] Summary, Meuse-Argonne, Sept. 21-Nov. 20, 1918.

[666] Cheseldine, *Ohio in the Rainbow*, 254.

[667] Sterner, *CADSC*, III, 365.

[668] Sterner, II, 102.

[669] H. H. Grave Correspondence with ABMC October 11, 1926, MAMA, RG-15, Box 35-41, Folder 5.

[670] Cheseldine, *Ohio in the Rainbow*, 253.

[671] Straub, *Sergeant's Diary*, 197.

[672] Reilly, *Americans All*, 657.

[673] Taber, *Story of the 168th*, 179.

[674] Taber, 179.

[675] NARA RG 120 Records of Combat Divisions 42nd Division, 151st FA Regt., Box 41, ARC ID 301641, Entry NM-9` 1241.

[676] Sterner, *CADSC* IV, 236-237.

[677] Taber, *Story of the 168th*, 184.

[678] Reilly, *Americans All*, 653.

[679] Pershing, *My Experiences*, 336.

[680] Pershing, 336; War Diary of the 166th Infantry, reported verbatim in Cheseldine, *Ohio in the Rainbow*, 250-253; 256.

[681] Summerall, *Way of Duty*, 144-145.

[682] Yockelson, *Forty-Seven Days*, 104.

[683] Collins, *History of the 151st*, 148.

[684] Cheseldine, *Ohio in the Rainbow*, 246-254.

[685] A caisson is a large, wooden crate on wheels; soldiers used these to transport ammunition. Bjork, *Harness & Hitch*, 183.

[686] Bjork, 184.

[687] Reilly, *Americans All*, 658.

[688] Reilly, 659.

[689] Reilly, 659-680.

[690] Reilly, 678.

[691] Wright, *Meuse Argonne Diary*, 52.

[692] Amerine, *Alabama's Own in France*, 162.

[693] Wheeler, *Big Red One*, 89.

[694] Amerine, *Alabama's Own in France*, 180.

[695] Reilly, *Americans All*, 712.

[696] N.P. Parkinson and Joel R. Parkinson ed., *Commanding Fire*, 154.

[697] George McIntosh Sparks, Walter Alexander Harris, Cooper Winn and J.A. Moss, *Macon War's Work*, 102.

[698] Reilly, *Americans All*, 712.

[699] ABMC file on C/168th Infantry, 42nd Division, Box 233, RG 117, letter #6, W. R. Witherell, October 8, 1926.

[700] Taber, *Story of the 168th*, 182.

[701] Taber, 182.

[702] NARA RG 120, Records of Combat Divisions 42nd Division, Letter # 6 Correspondence of ABMC with Charles Seeley dated December 3, 1924, A-714, 2-M M/A.

[703] Written in longhand by Lieutenant W. R. Witherell on ABMC mimeographed 1st revision dated September 30, 1929. RG 117, Correspondence of former division officers, Box 233, file 7147-M/MA, Entry No. H 31.

[704] Amerine, *Alabama's Own in France*, 196.

[705] Sterner, *CADSC*, III, 294. Nelson, who had earned a DSC for action near the Croix Rouge Farm on July 26, earned two (First and Second Oak Leaf Cluster) for his October 16 actions at the Côte de Châtillon.

[706] Taber, *Story of the 168th*, 199.

[707] Letter from 2nd Lt. Carl Wingerson to ABMC dated 4-11-29, RG 117, Correspondence of former division officers, Box 233, file 7147-M/MA, Entry No. H 31.

[708] Reilly, *Americans All*, 684.

[709] Sterner, *CADSC*, II, 251-252; Drouhin family papers, courtesy of his son, Mr. Robert Drouhin, Beaune, France. Drouhin was also awarded the Distinguished Service Medal of the US Army on December 26, 1918, in orders signed by Brig. Gen., General Staff, Douglas MacArthur. The award recognized Drouhin's service as a French Army Officer attached first as a Senior Instructor to the 167th Infantry Regiment in Lorraine and as a Senior French Officer in the 84th Brigade from the fighting in the Champagne through all subsequent combat until the capture of the Côte de Châtillon on October 16, 1918. Drouhin and MacArthur maintained a friendship and correspondence for four decades after the war, after Drouhin returned to his family wine business.

[710] Sterner, *CADSC*, III, 328.

[711] Sterner, IV, 159.

[712] Sterner, II, 26.

[713] RG 117, Correspondence of former division officers, Box 233, file 7147-M/MA, Entry No. H 31.

[714] Sterner, *CADSC*, II, 28.

[715] Reilly, *Americans All*, 685; Sherman L. Fleek, *Place the Headstones*, 15.

[716] ABMC file 714.2-M/MA, F- 167th Infantry, 42nd Division, Meuse Argonne Operations. Letter #6, checked May 4, 1927.

[717] Reilly, *Americans All*, 685; ABMC file F-167th Infantry, 42nd Division, Box 232, RG 117, Meuse Argonne Operations. Checked July 21, 1930, Capt. Carl Wingerson.

[718] Reilly, *Americans All*, 685.

[719] Sterner, *CADSC*, II, 282-283.

[720] Royal Little Correspondence with ABMC November 26, 1926, MAMA, RG-15, Box 75, Folder 5.

[721] Reilly, *Americans All*, 718-719; George E. Leach, *War Diary*, 141.

[722] Collins, *History of the 151st*, 149.

[723] Ferrell, *Question of MacArthur's Reputation*, 62.

[724] MAMA, Telegram from General Menoher, Headquarters 42nd Division, 26 October 1918 to General Summerall, Commanding General V Army Corps.

[725] Reilly, *Americans All*, 733.

[726] Taber, *Story of the 168th*, 207.

[727] Ferrell, *Question of MacArthur's Reputation,* 7.

[728] Reilly, *Americans All*, 766.

[729] George Herbert, *Challenge of War*, 121.

[730] Reilly, *Americans All*, 640.

[731] Marguerie's brother, Henri, served in WWII as commander of the French 1st Armored Division in 1945. He continued serving with the French military in Indochina (present-day Vietnam) and Algeria. His son is the present owner of the Chateau de Cornay.

[732] Excerpts from the unpublished memoirs of Marguerite de Pouilly, courtesy of Martine de Pouilly. Translated from the original French by Dr. Monique B. Seefried.

BIBLIOGRAPHY

The bibliography includes all the major archival groups and other materials used in researching this book. The footnotes include detailed references for each archival source. In the case of other materials, only the short citation appears in the footnote. References employ the following abbreviations.

ADAH Alabama Department of Archives and History, Montgomery, AL

AEF American Expeditionary Forces

AFB Air Force Base

AMHI Army Military History Institute, Carlisle Barracks, Carlisle, PA

GPO Government Printing Office

MAMA MacArthur Memorial Archives, Norfolk, VA

MCoE Maneuver Center of Excellence, Donovan Research Library, Fort Benning, GA

NARA National Archives and Records Administration (US)

SHD/DAT Service Historique de la Défense, Vincennes, France

UNLA University of Nebraska–Lincoln, Archives and Special Collections

USMA United States Military Academy, West Point, NY

Archival Materials

Auburn University Special Collections and Archives, Auburn, AL
Wren, Edward R. Collection. *Letters.*

Army Military History Institute, Carlisle Barracks, Carlisle, PA (AMHI)
Correspondence, First Division Headquarters. Captain William Haselton.
Summaries -- Meuse-Argonne –Sept. 21, 1918 – Nov. 20. 1918, Summaries of Intelligence 5th Army Corps.
World War I Veterans Survey. 1st Division. Pvt. Elvid B. Johnson,

medic, 2nd Machine Gun Battalion. Earl R. Poorbaugh, 26th Infantry Regiment.

MacArthur Memorial Archives, Norfolk, VA (MAMA)
Royal Little Correspondence with ABMC.

Maneuver Center of Excellence, Donovan Research Library, Fort Benning, GA (MCoE)
http://www.benning.army.mil/library/content/Virtual/Donovan papers/wwi/

Bonney, Frank E. *Operations of the Thirty-Fifth Division in the First Phase of the Meuse Argonne,* Advanced Officers' Course, 1922-23. The Infantry School, Fort Benning.

Boyd, Leonard R. *Operations of the 1st Bn, 16th Inf. In the 2nd phase of the Meuse-Argonne.* Company Officers' Course, 1924-25, The Infantry School, Fort Benning.

Caffey, B.F. *The Operations of the 1st Division in the 2nd Phase of the Meuse-Argonne.* Company Officers' Course, 1924-25, The Infantry School, Fort Benning.

Cornish, George R. F. *The First Division US in the Second Phase of the Meuse-Argonne Offensive, October 4-31, 1918.* Advanced Course, 1928-29, The Infantry School, Fort Benning.

Forster, George J. *Operations of the 37mm Platoon, 26th Infantry,* Advanced Course, 1931-32, The Infantry School, Fort Benning.

Frasier, Lyman S. *Operations of the Third Battalion, 26th Infantry, First Division, in the Second and Third Phases of the Meuse-Argonne Offensive,* Advanced Course, 1926-27, The Infantry School, Fort Benning.

Gillette, A. Ward. *Historical Tactical Study, The Meuse-Argonne Offensive – First Phase, Sept. 26-Oct.3, 1918, An Attack of a Defensive Zone.* Regular Course, 1936-37, The Infantry School, Fort Benning.

Helsley, Albert B. *Operations of the Machine Gun Company, 16th Infantry, (1st Infantry Division), during the Second Phase, Meuse-Argonne Offensive, September 30-October 12, 1918 (personal experience)*. Advanced Course, 1930-31, The Infantry School, Fort Benning.

Legge, Barnwell R. *The 1st Division in the Meuse-Argonne, Sept. 26 to Oct. 12, 1918*. Advanced Course, 1922-1923, The Infantry School, Fort Benning.

McLain, Ralph E. *Organization and Operations of the Division Trains, lst Div., December 1917-January 1919*. Advanced Officers Class, 1922-23, The Infantry School, Fort Benning.

Stark, John V. *3rd Battalion, 140th Infantry, 35th Division in the Meuse-Argonne, Sept. 26-Oct. 5, 1918*. Advanced Course, 1926-27, The Infantry School, Fort Benning.

Rutherford B. Hayes Presidential Library
Correspondence of Dalton Hayes.

National Archives and Records Administration (US). National Archives Building, College Park, MD (NARA)
RG 117, Correspondence with the American Battle Monuments Commission.
RG 120, World War I Organization Records, Entry 1241.
1st Division (Box 66).
42nd Division (Boxes 35-41).
RG 165, German Military Records 1917-1919, Entry 320.

USMA United States Military Academy Library (USMA) Special Collections
930 USMA 1886, Papers Concerning 42nd Division File, Menoher File, Colonel Castle WWI File.

Books and Articles

Abbot, William J. *The United States in The Great War*. New York: Leslie-Judge Co., 1919.

American Battle Monuments Commission (ABMC). *1st Division, Summary of Operations in the World War*. Washington, DC: GPO, 1944.

———. *35th Division, Summary of Operations in the World War.* Washington, DC: GPO, 1944.

———. *42nd Division, Summary of Operations in the World War.* Washington, DC: GPO, 1944.

———. *American Armies and Battlefields in Europe.* Washington, DC: GPO, 1938.

American Decorations: a list of awards of the Congressional Medal of Honor, the Distinguished-Service Cross, and the Distinguished-Service Medal; awarded under authority of the Congress of the United States, 1862-1926. Compiled in the Office of the Adjutant General of the Army and published by order of the Secretary of War. Washington: U.S. Government Printing Office, 1927.

Amerine, William H. *Alabama's Own in France.* New York: Eaton & Gettinger, 1919.

Belmonte, Peter L. *Days of Perfect Hell.* Atglen, PA: Schiffer Publishing Ltd., 2015.

Bjork, Eskil I. *Harness & Hitch, a Diary. Battery F 149th Field Artillery, Rainbow Division, En route to the Argonne.* 1935.

Bowman, Stephen L. *A Century of Valor.* Wheaton, IL: Cantigny First Division Foundation, 2004.

Braim, Paul F. *The Test of Battle: The American Expeditionary Forces in the Meuse Argonne Campaign.* 1987; reprint, Shippensburg, PA: White Mane Books, 1998.

Brouillon, Louis. *L'Argonne, Guide du Touriste et du Promeneur, 1907,* reprint. Paris: Le Livre d'Histoire, 1999.

Bullard, Robert Lee, in collaboration with Earl Reeves. *American Soldiers Also Fought, American Soldiers Also Fought.* New York: Longmans Green & Co., 1936.

Chastaine, Ben. *History of the 18th U.S. Infantry.* Hyman's Publishing, 1919.

Cheseldine, R. M. *Ohio in the Rainbow, Official Story of the 166th Infantry 42nd Division in the World War.* Columbus, OH: F. J. Heer Printing, 1924.

Clay, Steven E. *Blood and Sacrifice, The History of The 16th Infantry Regiment.* Chicago: Cantigny First Division Foundation, 2001.

Cochrane, Rexmond C. *The Use of Gas in the Meuse-Argonne Campaign of September-November, 1918*. US Army Chemical Corps, Historical Studies, Gas Warfare in World War I, Study Number 10. Washington, DC: US Army Chemical Corps, Historical Office, 1958.

Collins, Louis, L. *History of the 151st Field Artillery, Rainbow Division*. Vol. 1. Edited by Wayne E. Stevens. St. Paul: Minnesota War Records Commission, 1924.

Crocker, H.W. *The Yanks are Coming: A Military History of World War I*. Washington, DC: Regnery Publishing, 2014.

Doll, F. S. *1st Division, Meuse-Argonne Offensive 1-13 October 1918, Measures to Gain Surprise*. The Command and General Staff School, Fort Leavenworth, KS, 1931-1932.

Duffy, Francis P. *Father Duffy's Story*. Garden City, NY: George H. Doran, Country Life Press, 1919.

Eddy, M.S. *A Critical Analysis of the German Operations Opposed to the Americans from Oct. 1-11, 1918*. The Command and General Staff School, Fort Leavenworth, KS, Second Year Course, 1933-1934.

Eggleston, Michael A. *The 5th Marine Regiment Devils Dogs in World War I*. Jefferson, NC: McFarland & Company, Inc, 2016.

Eisenhower, John S. D. *Yanks: The Epic Story of the American Army in World War I*. New York: Free Press, 2001.

Ferrell, Robert H. *America's Deadliest Battle: Meuse-Argonne, 1918*. Lawrence: University Press of Kansas, 2007.

———. *Collapse at Meuse-Argonne*. Columbia, MO: University of Missouri Press, 2004.

———. *The Question of MacArthur's Reputation: Côte de Châtillon, October 14–16, 1918*. Columbia: University of Missouri Press, 2008.

Fivecoat, David G. *Fine Conduct Under Fire: The Tactical Effectiveness of the 165th Infantry Regiment in the First World War*. US Army Command and General Staff College. Fort Leavenworth, KS, 2004.

Fleek, Sherman L. *Place the Headstones Where They Belong*. Logan: Utah State University Press, 2008.

Ford, Nancy Gentile. *Americans All! Foreign-Born Soldiers in World War I*. College Station: Texas A&M University Press, 2001.

Frazer, Nimrod T. *Send the Alabamians, World War I Fighters in the Rainbow Division*. Tuscaloosa: University of Alabama Press, 2014.

Fullerton, Charles B. *The Twenty-Sixth Infantry in France by the Regimental Adjutant*. Montabaur – Frankfurt: Printing Office Martin Flock & Co. G.M.B.H., 1919.

George, Herbert. *The Challenge of War*. New York: Vantage Press, 1966.

Goerlitz, Walter, ed. *The Kaiser and his Court, The Diaries, Note Books and Letters of Admiral George Alexander von Mueller, Chief of the Naval Cabinet*. New York: Harcourt, Brace & World Inc., 1964.

Grotelueschen, Mark Ethan. *The AEF Way of War: The American Army and Combat in World War I*. New York: Cambridge University Press, 2007.

Guelton, Frédéric "Les opérations entre Meuse et Argonne, Septembre-Novembre, 1919" in *Du Sergent York à Patton: Les Américains dans la Meuse, 1917-1919*, Société des Lettres, Sciences et Arts de Bar le Duc, 1988.

Hallas, James, H. *Doughboy War: The American Expeditionary Force in World War I*. 2000; reprint, Mechanicsburg, PA: Stackpole Books, 2009.

Harbord, James G. *American Army in France, 1917-1919* (Little Brown & Co., Boston, 1936).

Harter, Hélène. *Les Etats-Unis dans la Grande Guerre*. Paris: Tallandier, 2017.

Hartzell, Arthur. *Meuse-Argonne Battle (Sept. 26-Nov.11, 1918)*. Nabu Public Domain Reprints, 2014.

History of the First Division during the World War 1917-1919, Compiled and published by The Society of The First Division. First Ed. Philadelphia, PA: The John C. Winston Company 1922.

History of the 2nd Machine Gun Battalion. New York: Hymans Publishing Co., 1920.

Hogan, Martin. *The Shamrock Battalion of Rainbow, A Story of the "Fighting Sixty-Ninth."* New York: D. Appleton and Company, 1919.

Jeanneney, Jean-Noël. *Jours de Guerre 1914-1918, Les Trésors des Archives Photographiques du Journal* Excelsior. Les Arènes, 2013.

Johnson, Douglas Wilson. *Battlefields of the World War, Western and Southern Fronts.* New York: Oxford University Press, 1921.

Kenamore, Clair. *From Vauquois Hill to Exermont, a History of the Thirty-Fifth Division of the United States Army.* St. Louis: Guard Publishing Co., 1919.

Kyler, Donald. *The Thoughts & Memories of a Common Soldier by a former member of G Company, 16th Infantry.* Copyright registration number TXu 431792, August 16, 1990. AMHI.

Langille, Leslie. *Men of the Rainbow.* Chicago: The O'Sullivan Publishing House, 1933.

Leach, George E. *War Diary.* Minneapolis: Pioneer Printers, 1923.

— — —. *The 1st Division in the Meuse-Argonne, Sept. 26 to Oct. 12, 1918.* Monographs of The World War. The Infantry School.

Lenahan, John C. *Analysis to the 35th Division's Application of Operational Art During World War I.* School of Advanced Military Studies, United States Army Command and Staff College. Fort Leavenworth, KS: 2017.

Lengel, Edward G., Ed. *A Companion to the Meuse-Argonne Campaign.* Chichester, West Sussex: Wiley Blackwell, 2014.

Lengel, Edward G. *To Conquer Hell, The Meuse-Argonne, 1918, The Epic Battle that Ended the First World War.* New York: Henry Holt & Cy, LLC, 2009.

Liggett, Hunter. *Commanding an American Army.* Boston & New York: Houghton Mifflin Company, 1925.

Lloyd, Nick. *Hundred Days, The Campaign that Ended World War I.* New York: Basic Books, 2014.

MacArthur, Douglas. *Reminiscences.* 1964; reprint. Annapolis, MD: Bluejacket Books, Naval Institute Press, 2001.

McHenry, Herbert B. *As A Private Saw It.* Indiana, PA: The A.G. Halldin Publishing Co., 1977.

Mansfield, William A. *Diary of a Shavetail*.
http://www.tallisfamily.co.uk/ShavetailDiary.htm.

Marshall, George C. *Memoirs of my Services in the World War, 1917–1918*. Boston: Houghton Mifflin Company, 1976.

Mead, Gary. *The Doughboys, America and the First World War*. New York: The Overlook Press, 2000.

Metcalf, James. *Operations of the 1st Corps, Second Phase of the Meuse–Argonne*, Monographs of the World War, The Infantry School, 543-547.

Meyer, C. G. *The World Remade, America in World War I*. New York: Bantam Books, 2016.

Miller, Henry Russell. *The First Division*. Pittsburgh: The Crescent Press, 1920.

Millett, Allan R. *The General, Robert L. Bullard, and Officership in the United States Army, 1881–1925*. Westport, CT: Greenwood Press, 1975.

Order of Battle of the United States Land Forces in the World War. American Expeditionary Forces: Divisions. Washington, DC: Center of Military History, United States Army, 1988. Last updated 29 July 2016.
https://history.army.mil/html/bookshelves/collect/oob_us_lf_w wi_1917-1919.html.

Palmer, Frederick. *Our Greatest Battle: Meuse Argonne*. New York: Dodd, Mead and Company, 1919.

Parkinson N.P., and Parkinson Joel R. ed. *Commanding Fire: An Officer's Life in the 151st Machine Gun Battalion, 42nd Rainbow Division During World War I*. Atglen, PA: Schiffer Publishing, Ltd. 2014.

Parschall, Rod. *The Defeat of Imperial Germany 1917-1918*. Chapel Hill, NC: Algonquin Books of Chapel Hill, 1989.

Pershing, John J. *Final Report*. Washington, DC: GPO, 1920.

———. *My Experiences in the World War*. Vol. 2. New York: Frederick A. Stokes, 1931.

Reilly, Henry J. *Americans All: The Rainbow at War; Official History of the 42nd Rainbow Division in the World War*. Columbus, OH: The F. J. Heer Printing Co. Publishers, 1936.

Reynolds, Francis J. *The Story of The Great War*. VIII. New York: P. F. Collier & Son, 1920.

Sparks, George McIntosh, Walter Alexander Harris, Cooper Winn, and J. A. Moss. *Macon War's Work: A History of Macon in the Great World War*. Edited by George Sparks. Macon, GA: The J. W. Burke Company, n.d.

Sterner, C. Douglas. ed. *Citations for Awards of The Distinguished Service Cross*. Volumes I-IV. Copyright 2006, Updated 2008.

Stewart, Lawrence O. *Rainbow Bright*. Philadelphia: Dorrance Publishers, 1923.

The Story of The Twenty-Eighth Infantry in The Great War. American Expeditionary Forces, 1919.

Straub, Elmer Frank. *A Sergeant's Diary in the World War: The Diary of an Enlisted Member of the 150th Field Artillery. October 27, 1917 to August 7, 1919*. Indianapolis: Indiana Historical Commission, 1923.

Strohn, Matthias, Ed. *World War I Companion*. Osprey Publishing, 2013.

Summerall, Charles Pelot. *The Way of Duty, Honor, Country*. Lexington: University Press of Kentucky, 2010.

Taber, John H. *The Story of the 168th Infantry*. 2 vol. Iowa City: State Historical Society of Iowa, 1925.

United States in World War I, Organization of the American Expeditionary Forces, Center for Military History, 1988.

Van Ells, Mark D. *America and World War I, A Traveler's Guide*. Northhampton, MA: Interlink Books, 2015.

Venzon, Ann Cipriano, Ed. *The United States in the First World War: An Encyclopedia*. New York: Garland, 1915.

Weed, Earl H. *The Story of the Sixteenth Infantry in France by the Regimental Chaplain*. Frankfurt, Germany: Martin Flock, 1919.

Weingartner, Steven. *Blue Spaders, The 16th Infantry Regiment 1917-1967*. Wheaton: Cantigny Military History Series, 1997.

Wheeler, James Scott. *The Big Red One: America's Legendary 1st Infantry Division from World War I to Desert Storm*. Modern War Studies. Lawrence, KS: University Press of Kansas, 2007.

Wright, William W. *Meuse Argonne Diary, A Division Commander in World War I*. Edited by Robert H. Ferrell. Columbia: University of Missouri Press, 2004.

Yockelson, Mitchell. *Forty-Seven Days, How Pershing's Warriors Came of Age to Defeat the German Army in World War I*. New York: New American Library, 2016.

Newspapers

Army and Navy Journal

INDEX